D0763433

Wild Weekends in
Utah

Wild Weekends in
Utah

AN OUTDOOR ADVENTURE GUIDE

Lori Lee

The Countryman Press
Woodstock, Vermont

Library of Congress Cataloging-in-Publication Data has been applied for.

ISBN 0-88150-653-2

Book design by Hespenheide Design
Maps by Paul Woodward, © The Countryman Press
Cover photo © Russ Bishop
Interior photographs by the author

Published by The Countryman Press, P.O. Box 748, Woodstock, Vermont 05091
Distributed by W.W. Norton & Company, Inc., 500 Fifth Avenue, New York, NY 10110

Printed in the United States of America

10 9 8 7 6 5 4 3 2 1

Dedication

To God, the master creator of a world so lovely and artistic we are drawn to constant wonder and worship. In the simple words of Joyce Kilmer in his poem "Trees," "Poems are made by fools like me, But only God can make a tree."

Acknowledgments

Thanks to everyone who explored the wonderful wild places of Utah with me. Thanks to Glen Spencer for sharing his knowledge of some of the best Utah has to offer, for his untiring, selfless efforts in editing, and for his advice. Thanks to the guides, such as Sheri Griffith Expeditions, Wild Rivers, Tag-a-Long, and Tex's Riverways, for sharing their knowledge of the Utah waterways and for showing me things one can only see from the river.

Thanks also to Rebecca Thalman for her editing help, to my children for letting me leave so often, to my parents for their support, to iGage Mapping Corporation for sharing their software, and last but not least, thank you to Helen Whybrow for starting me down the path that would lead to so many adventures.

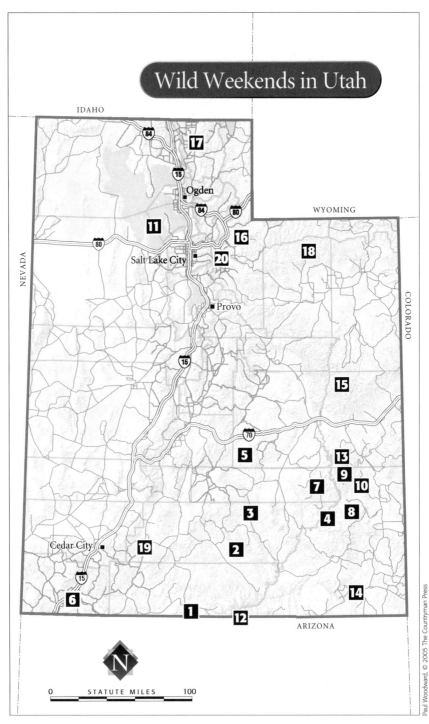

Wild Weekends in Utah

IDAHO

NEVADA

WYOMING

COLORADO

ARIZONA

Ogden

Salt Lake City

Provo

Cedar City

N

STATUTE MILES

0   100

Contents

DESERT

WATER

MOUNTAINS

Colorful cliff in the San Rafael Swell area

Introduction

The state of Utah is unlike any other place on the planet. It's a terrain that begs for outdoor sports enthusiasts—and they come. Whether you prefer a tree-lined hiking trail or a desert river path, a canoe paddle down a twisting waterway or a kayaking foray into hidden red rock canyons, an adrenalin-driven rush down single-track mountain bike trails, or first tracks down Utah's famous feather-light powder, Utah holds adventure possibilities at every turn. Home to the 2002 Winter Olympics, Utah proved it had the terrain, facilities, and spirit to play host to the world.

But there's a wonderful side of Utah the Olympic attendees never saw. Even after months of traveling through the most wild and beautiful areas of the state, my appreciation and awe of the towering, multicolored canyon walls, the fresh greenness of the mountains, and the rivers both clear and silty only grew more profound. No matter how many times I drive by the bizarre bulbous formations of the San Rafael Reef, it will never become ordinary.

Utah is incredibly diverse. The unparalleled starkness and grandeur of canyon walls that reach thousands of feet into the sky stand in contrast to the glistening alpine peaks of the Wasatch and Bear River Ranges. And the rivers, regarded as some of the West's most precious resources, flow down from the mountains clear and cold or traverse the parched desert lowlands like sinuous brown snakes. Red, orange, brown, and white cliffs paint a rainbow on the landscape; mesas, buttes, pinnacles, goblins, mazes, chutes, and plateaus add dimension to this unique part of the country; and mountains, lakes, rivers, and streams bring it to life.

Heading into the backcountry is about freedom, about escaping the tedium of modern life, about recreation and reconnection with the spiritual essence we find in remote wilderness. With technologically advanced gear and a societal shift toward outdoor recreation, mainstream America has begun to binge on a wide range of outdoor adventure sports. This means that more people than ever are looking for ways to enjoy the backcountry—but where to go?

The idea for this book came about as I labored to plan the next outdoor adventure for myself, my husband, and a couple of close friends. We had only limited time to backpack, climb, and raft—things we couldn't do with our young children in tow. As we had to maximize our time, weekends away often involved more than just one sport. We found that we really liked going to one place and participating in a variety of sports. If we went to Zion National Park we would descend a classic slot canyon one day, and then pedal the renowned mountain bike trails in the area the next.

During years of arranging such trips, I noticed that the only guidebooks available were dedicated to one type of sport. There was no information on the best multi-sport recreation in Utah, or any other state for that matter. For each trip I planned, I was forced to buy a variety of books, track down numerous phone numbers, and consult different maps. It was a tedious process. I had to figure out where to camp, whether I needed advance reservations, which trails were worth the time, how to find the trailheads, and what permits might be necessary. So simplifying the preparation and maximizing the activities on weekend adventures was the impetus for this guide.

Utah's excellence as a multi-sport destination starts with geology. The state has three distinct geological zones: the Colorado Plateau, the Rocky Mountains, and the Great Basin. The only other state that can

A high-country waterfall in the Uintah Range

make a similar claim is New Mexico. These zones provide a diverse range of scenery and topography. Red rock slots, hoodoos, shifting sand dunes, towering buttes, a salt lake, desert waterways, thick alpine forests, red sandstone amphitheaters, two dozen peaks over 13,000 feet, and in winter, the best snow on earth—Utah has something for everyone.

In elevation alone Utah's terrain varies 11,000 feet, or two vertical miles. Because it is renowned for the red rock canyons in the southern part of the state, where most of the national parks are located, the impressive mountain ranges are often overlooked.

The Wasatch Mountains are a 200-mile-long range that holds the majority of the state's commercial ski areas, a large chunk of its rock climbing, and an array of alpine mountain biking. The Uintah Range, one of the few ranges in the country that runs east to west, dominates the northeast corner of the state. One hundred and fifty miles long, this range is home to Utah's tallest peaks and its most lush alpine forests.

Kings Peak, the highest point in the state at 13,528 feet (see chapter 18), includes a hike past amazing lakes and alpine waterfalls, and comes with bragging rights to having scaled the tallest peak in Utah.

The town of Brian Head is 9,700 feet above sea level and provides some of the state's best downhill mountain biking trails (see chapter 19). You can't say you've mountain biked Utah until you've been to Brian Head.

Lake Powell (see chapter 12) is the biggest reservoir in the state, capable of holding more than 25 million acre-feet of water. Touring kayaks can convey paddlers into miles of awe-inspiring canyons lined with towering sandstone walls and sandy beaches for camping.

Wild Weekends in Utah is the book I've wished I had a hundred times over the years. It gives the recreationalist 20 of the best weekend multi-sport adventures in one of the most beautiful and scenic states in the country. Not every adventure includes more than one sport, of course, as some require the entire weekend, but you'll find a variety of outdoor activities here. They span the entire state and incorporate the best mountain biking, river-running, backpacking, canyoneering, and canoeing to be had. Many adventures require an intermediate skill level, meaning that novices should come well prepared. But, as always, the level of difficulty must be gauged on an individual basis.

I have personally driven the roads, ridden the trails, backpacked the routes, and logged all the information for each of these weekend adventures, so you don't have to waste hours in planning. From packing recommendations to must-see sites along the trail, each chapter is a complete information source. If you want to head out for the adventure of a lifetime but only have the weekend in which to do it, this guide is for you.

A SHORT HISTORY

Home to two of the largest dinosaur graveyards in North America, Utah tells a story that begins over 500 million years ago. Dinosaur National Monument and the Cleveland-Lloyd Quarry supply fossils to museums

Ancient prints in the sandstone near the San Juan River

and universities around the world. Ancient Lake Bonneville, which is believed to have originated during the last ice age, once covered most of Utah and parts of Idaho and Nevada. Today, the Great Salt Lake is the remnant of that massive inland sea and is still the largest natural lake west of the Mississippi.

The earliest evidence of human habitation in the state is found in caves. Flint points, knives, and tools dated at 10,000 years old were left behind by primitive hunters. Nearly 2,000 years ago, hunter-gatherer tribes farmed the southern Utah valleys and prospered for almost 1,300 years before abruptly abandoning their homes for reasons that remain a mystery.

The Ute, Paiute, Goshute, and Shoshone tribes were present in the 19th century when European settlers blazed their trails into Utah. Trappers and mountain men also explored the state, mapping routes and collecting fur from the abundant wildlife. Their trails were followed by Mormon pioneers, as well as adventurers heading to the west coast. In the 1840s, John C. Fremont began his explorations of the area. His work, along with John Wesley Powell's, has supplied much of the information we have on conditions in what would become the state of Utah.

In 1847 the Mormon prophet Brigham Young, looking for a place of refuge where his people could escape the religious persecution they had received in the East, entered the Salt Lake Valley with a company of pioneers. As he looked down into the desert valley below, he declared, "This is the place." Zion, a Hebrew word meaning "a place of refuge or sanctuary," was established and Mormon followers from around the world began their pilgrimage to Utah to live together in community.

They immediately set to work planting crops and organizing what would become Salt Lake City. They developed an ingenious irrigation system that made the desert "blossom like the rose," and soon they were widely known for their work ethic and resourcefulness. Before long they had established a territorial government, built a theatre, started a newspaper, and built homes and forts, settlements and churches across the state. Utah was granted statehood in 1896.

Salt Lake City is still the home of the international church headquarters for the Mormons, or The Church of Jesus Christ of Latter-Day

Saints (LDS). Located along the Wasatch Front, the area where most of the state's population resides, Salt Lake City is a hub of culture, education, and religion. Temple Square hosts the famous Salt Lake Temple, the Tabernacle (home of the world-renowned Mormon Tabernacle Choir), two modern visitors' centers, and Church organizational buildings. Visitors are welcomed. Today over 70 percent of Utah's residents are members of the LDS Church, but in Salt Lake Valley 30 different denominations also meet weekly with every major world religion represented.

The state has many universities, and the young population is well educated. Salt Lake is an attractive location in part because it has such an array of amazing outdoor recreation in such close proximity to good cultural and educational opportunities.

LEAVE NO TRACE

Gone are the days when collecting firewood around your campsite is always acceptable. Gone are the days when leaving that biodegradable fruit peel is considered harmless. Gone are the days when backcountry visitors can casually approach the land through which they travel. With wilderness use growing and more and more people looking for solace in the canyons, mountains, and waterways of the natural world, there is no longer room for those unwilling to preserve the beauty of wild places.

The Leave No Trace (LNT) concept originated in the United States as a way to help the ever-growing tide of recreationalists minimize their impact. Land managers are banking on this education process to help protect public lands, and outdoor enthusiasts and nature lovers everywhere are learning and implementing the techniques necessary to keep the land and ecosystems as pristine as possible. The LNT practices are based on the idea of extending common courtesy to others who will follow, as well as to the flora and fauna in the areas we visit.

Utah is a magical but delicate land of canyons, sand dunes, mountains, deeply carved arroyos, prehistoric ruins, pictographs, petroglyphs, and cryptobiotic soil crusts. The extreme temperatures and aridity in these lands protect and preserve both the good and the bad. Corncobs

and pottery shards that are hundreds of years old can still be found at ancient Native American sites in the desert regions. But the climate that slows the breakdown of these items also slows the disintegration of human waste, litter, and unsightly markings. Because every wild area is unique, each has different guidelines for leaving no trace.

PACK IT IN, PACK IT OUT You've heard the mantra. It's easy enough. Anything you take in, you must pack out. Be prepared with garbage bags and resealable bags so that you can pack things out in the cleanest possible way. All food scraps, garbage, grease, leftovers, toilet paper, fishing line, etc. must be carried out with you.

TRAVEL AND CAMP ON DURABLE SURFACES To reduce damage to desert surfaces—many of which require hundreds of years to repair themselves—stay on established trails and in established campsites. Gravel, sand, or expanses of rock are good options for setting up a LNT camp. Walk single-file on trails rather than side by side to avoid widening routes. Don't bushwhack between campsites or undertake major remodel jobs when setting up camp. Breaking tree branches off a live tree leaves scars and opens the tree to disease.

Avoid creating new trails, fire rings, or campsites, and when you break camp make sure you have cleaned out all trash and removed all other evidence that you were there, which includes returning rocks and logs to their original positions and brushing out social trails.

PROTECT WATER RESOURCES Water forms and defines our landscape. It is powerful, and in the desert it is scarce. Campers need to respect water sources and make every effort to conserve them and keep them clean. A good general rule is to establish camp 200 feet from any water source. Animals need undisturbed access to water, and such a distance makes it less likely that humans will unintentionally contaminate the water.

San Juan River

When defecating, make sure that cat holes are 6 to 8 inches deep and at least 200 feet from any water source. Urinate well away from camps and trails, and aim for rocks or sand rather than vegetation, as salt-deprived animals have been known to defoliate plants that have been urinated on to get the salt. In desert river areas experts suggest that if no bathroom facilities are available it is best to urinate in the rivers. This keeps the heavily traveled riverbanks from smelling like outhouses. All solid waste should be packed out of these river corridors. And no matter where you're camping, toilet paper and feminine hygiene products should always to be packed out.

WASTEWATER AND FEEDING ANIMALS Use very small amounts of soap, if any, to wash yourself or your dishes, and dump dirty water 200 feet from the original water source. Hand sanitizers are a worthwhile option as they allow you to wash your hands without water.

Use a clean pot when collecting water for dishes. Carry it the required distance to keep from trampling the streambanks and polluting the source. When finished with the dishes, strain the water and pack out the food scraps. Don't leave food or food waste where animals can get it because it damages their health, alters natural behavior, and introduces unusual foods into their diet.

Bears offer a good example of wildlife behavior alterations in regard to human food. If wild bears aren't exposed to human food, they won't hang around campsites and garbage bins. But once they've had a taste they seek out humans and have been known to attack coolers, tents, and people. Rodents, birds, and skunks also get used to handouts and are drawn to human camps as a result of past experience. Animals are opportunists; don't give them the opportunity.

MINIMIZING CAMPFIRE IMPACT Campfires are no longer permitted in many areas, and you should always use established fire rings where fires are allowed. Fire pans are another way of making a low-impact fire, as is excavating a shallow depression in the sand or gravel at the bottom of a dry wash that has no organic soil. When you're finished, scatter the ash before refilling the depression. This will make the site less noticeable to others. If you're in an area where wood collecting is allowed, use smaller

Plan carefully for trips into remote country

pieces of wood that will burn completely to ash. Gather driftwood and deadwood where allowed. Never break limbs from live trees.

Other good backcountry ethics include being considerate of wildlife by watching from a distance and doing your best not to disturb their habitat. Remember to leave natural features undisturbed. Do not alter, or even touch, prehistoric sites you come across or take items you find as souvenirs. Do not carry out specimens or seeds, which may spread non-native plants and animals. Invasive species can take over areas when introduced into non-native ecosystems. Keep a low profile, be courteous, and don't disturb other visitors.

Like thousands of others, you love the land, love to be in it, and love to find solace and recreation in its natural boundaries. It is up to you to do your part and walk softly upon the places we all love.

HELPFUL HINTS

SELF-RELIANCE Adventuring in Utah requires careful preparation. Many areas are remote and the summer heat, especially in the desert, can be harsh. Always bring enough water and the correct clothing and gear. Check current weather conditions and flash flood potential when traveling in slot canyons. Thirty years ago Edward Abbey said, "The finest quality of this stone, these plants and animals, this desert landscape is the indifference manifest to our presence, our absence, our coming, our staying or our going. Whether we live or die is a matter of absolutely no concern whatsoever to the desert."

You are responsible for preparing for your time in the wilderness. Nothing—not a cell phone nor the best first-aid kit in the world—can compensate for poor judgment and planning. Many of the adventures listed here are far out of reach of quick rescue, and you need to be prepared to take care of yourself and those traveling with you.

NAVIGATION Global Positioning System (GPS) coordinates are included for routes where trails or points of interest are difficult to locate. By programming these coordinates into your GPS, you will be able to pinpoint specific trails, scenic arches, and campsites. It isn't necessary to have a GPS to enjoy the trips in this book, of course, but for those who have one the coordinates will provide extra assistance. Obviously, some of the canyons on these trips are too deep for a GPS, so coordinates are only given where satellite reception is possible.

DESERT ECOSYSTEMS AND CRYPTOBIOTIC SOIL The desert ecosystem is very fragile. The availability of water is what ultimately determines which plants and animals thrive in any given place. The rain that falls in the desert evaporates or drains quickly, yet some plants and animals are hardy enough to survive on amazingly little water. Though the soil may just resemble dirt, it is home to a wide variety of living organisms vital to the desert ecosystem.

If you look closely you'll see a crust that looks like a small colony of dark pinnacles growing out of the ground. This crust is known as cryptobiotic soil. It provides a framework upon which bacteria, the basic life forms of the desert, can grow. They are the foundation of life in the desert because of the key role they play in erosion control and water retention.

Unfortunately, human activities are harmful to the biological crusts. When you step on cryptobiotic soil, you are destroying a framework for life that may have taken hundreds of years to develop. Under good conditions a thin veneer may return in five years. In places of very low rainfall, it can take up to 250 years to return. For these reasons it is crucial that we are respectful of the ecosystem we are entering. Whether you're traveling on foot or by bike or 4×4, always stay on designated trails.

Desert

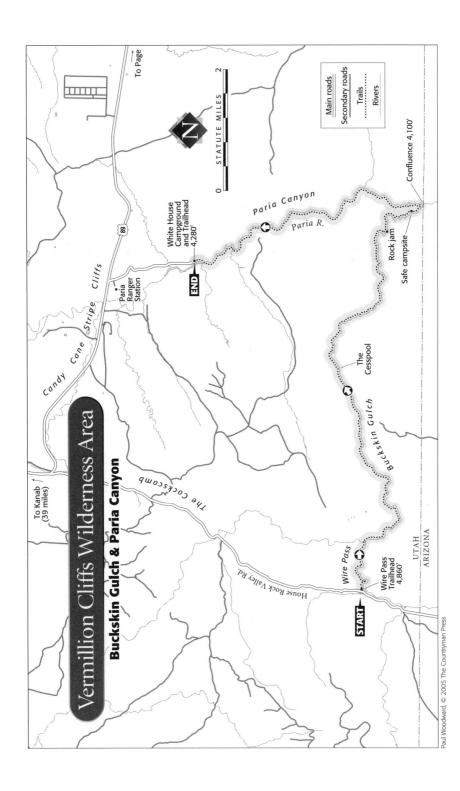

Vernillion Cliffs Wilderness Area

Buckskin Gulch & Paria Canyon

To Kanab
(39 miles)

Candy Cane Stripe Cliffs

To Page

89

Paria Ranger Station

White House Campground and Trailhead 4,280'

The Cockscomb

House Rock Valley Rd.

Wire Pass

Wire Pass Trailhead 4,860'

START

UTAH
ARIZONA

Buckskin Gulch

The Cesspool

END

Paria Canyon

Paria R.

Safe campsite

Rock jam

Confluence 4,100'

Main roads
Secondary roads
Trails
Rivers

N

0   1   2
STATUTE MILES

Paul Woodward, © 2005 The Countryman Press

Wire Pass

Paria Canyon–Vermillion Cliffs Wilderness Area

🚶 🧗 BUCKSKIN GULCH AND PARIA CANYON

The Prima Donna of Slot Canyons

Welcome to Utah's—or for that matter, the West's and possibly the world's—most striking slot canyon: Buckskin Gulch. Buckskin is the prized notch on any canyoneer's belt. Rumored to be the longest slot canyon in the world at 12 miles, Buckskin Gulch is a tributary of the Paria River. The Gulch is an alley of striking cliff walls from 18 inches to 50 feet apart that reach heights of 400 hundred feet on

3

average. The curved and colorful stone walls host a pastiche of hueco (rounded-out holes in a rock face) and contrasting linear block cuts. The geometry alone is worth the trip.

There is only one way in and one way to go until you reach the confluence with Paria Canyon, which is just as easy to navigate on the walk upriver.

Two major challenges arise in the Gulch: first, 1.5 hours of wading through stagnant pools that vary in depth according to previous rains and flooding, and second, a boulder jam with a 15-foot drop. The pools are scuzzy with gray-green mud, but that's part of the fun of canyoneering. The boulder jam requires either a Class 4 climb down Moki-like steps chiseled into a giant boulder or a rope descent. Otherwise, the canyon is non-technical, although the pools can be a challenge under certain conditions.

Buckskin Gulch is in the Paria Canyon–Vermillion Cliffs Wilderness Area, and the trail described here gives you the experience of the Buckskin as well as a section of the scenic Paria River itself. Conditions always affect the type of adventure you will have here, as lower water makes for an easier jaunt and higher water, a very intense journey. Regardless, a trip through Buckskin and up the Paria is a top-notch outdoor adventure with unparalleled scenery.

SPORT: Backpacking, canyoneering

RATING: Easy to moderate; the depth of the pools of water will determine the difficulty level

DISTANCE: 20.95 total miles one way; Wire Pass, 1.7 miles; Buckskin Gulch, 12 miles; Paria River, 7.25 miles

TIME: Two days

GETTING THERE: From Salt Lake City, head south on I-15 toward Las Vegas. After 213 miles take Exit 95, the junction with UT 20. Go east on

UT 20 for 20 miles, then turn right and follow US 89 for 10 miles. Turn left on East Center Street/US 89 in Panguitch and follow US 89 for 67 more miles to Kanab.

Continue on US 89 for 43 miles towards Page, Arizona. About 43 miles east of Kanab you cross the Paria River, where there is a sign directing you to the Paria Contact Station on your right. A graded road east of the ranger station takes you 2.1 miles to White House Campground. Leave your shuttle car in the parking lot here. (If you only have one vehicle you can also pay to be shuttled to the starting point.) Travel time is six hours, covering a total of 365 miles.

To reach the starting trailhead, travel 4.9 miles back toward Kanab from the Paria Contact Station to a dirt road named House Rock Valley Road. Turn left onto this road, on the west side of a bridge, which takes you to the Wire Pass Trailhead. House Rock Valley Road runs parallel to a formation called the Cockscomb, a scenic contrast of reds and greens. Follow this road for 8.5 miles to Wire Pass Trailhead. Parking is plentiful and vault toilets are available.

TRAIL: The trail begins and ends at established trailheads. Your starting point, Wire Pass Trailhead, is well-marked and has a clear footpath. Down trail, once you squeeze into Wire Pass itself, following the path entails staying in the narrow canyon and wash all the way to the White House Campground parking area at the other end.

Buckskin Gulch includes pools of water that range from calf-deep to a full swim. When you reach the Paria River confluence, the trail opens up and traces the riverbed. Turn left up the wash. Continue along the Paria until you reach a brown BLM trail marker on the right side of the river that marks the path to White House Campground and your car.

Flash flood danger within the Buckskin Gulch is no joke. Don't enter the canyon if rain is predicted. The ranger station has current weather and flash flood reports. Middle Trail is the only possible escape route within Buckskin Gulch, but the chances of being precisely at that spot when a flash flood hits are quite small. In a flash flood, the narrows can fill with sweeping waves of water within seconds. Stay away if thunderstorms are in the area.

Hiking Buckskin Gulch

If you're using a shuttle, have them transport you at the beginning of your hike rather than pick you up at the end. That way, if you're off schedule you aren't in danger of losing your ride or holding others up.

MAXIMUM GROUP SIZE: Parties are limited to no more than 10, with a total of 20 people allowed in from all trailheads each day.

CAMPING: Car camping is available at White House Campground, which has two pit toilets. No fires are allowed. Camping is on a first-come, first-served basis. There are picnic tables and barbeque grills at the sites, but no water is available unless the Paria is flowing.

Camping in the backcountry in Buckskin and Paria is the ultimate in Leave No Trace. Everything, and I mean *everything*, must be packed out. The BLM ranger at the Paria Contact Station will supply each person in your party with a silver disposable zipping waste bag in which you must deposit all human waste (to be carried out with you). No fires are allowed in the backcountry.

SEASON: March through May is prime hiking season, but the canyons are hikable spring, summer, and fall. The higher the water levels, the more difficult the canyons will be to navigate. During a cold, wet spell your chances of hypothermia increase because Buckskin Gulch is deep and shaded. If the pools are full you may have to swim in spots.

June and July are less crowded due to the warmer temperatures, but the Gulch provides enough shade that the only real sun exposure on this adventure will be during the hike up the Paria River later in the trip. In the past, July and August have posed the greatest thunderstorm and flash flood threat, but over the past few years—thanks to global warming—these months have proven to be equally pleasant.

PERMITS: A permit is required, and can be reserved on the Internet at www.az.blm.gov/paria/index2.html.

FEES: Five dollars per person, per day for your permit. Shuttle costs run approximately $60 for four people.

CLOTHING AND EQUIPMENT: You'll need two vehicles for this trip, or you can arrange to have your party shuttled. Bring dry bags to protect your belongings while wading through the pools of water. If the water is deep enough an inner tube will be helpful in floating your items across the pools as you swim, particularly if you don't have a dry bag large enough for all your gear. (The Paria Ranger Station will have the latest information on pool depth.)

A walking stick will help you feel your way through the pools of water in Buckskin and give you stability through the cobbles in Paria. Bring two pairs of shoes; I suggest hiking boots and water shoes. Sandals are okay for wading the pools, but small pebbles will find their way into them.

If you'll be hiking when the pools are more than knee high take plenty of warm clothes to put on when you exit the water. Going through the cold water with warm base layers and a hat will help you retain body heat.

The water in Buckskin is not potable, and even though springs do exist in the Gulch, you can't count on them. You will need to carry in all drinking water. A 30-foot rope for the descent from the boulder jam might come in handy as well.

SUGGESTED ITINERARY

DAY 1: Start the morning at the ranger station, where you can check the weather report and pick up your permit. Then leave one car at White House Campground and take another to the Wire Pass Trailhead, or take a shuttle.

The suggested trail begins at Wire Pass Trailhead, which takes you to Wire Pass via an open desert walk of 1.7 miles on a sandy trail and then down a wash. Once you enter the wash, don't take any footpaths that lead off to the right; stay in the wash. You'll know when you hit Wire Pass because the walls go up and you squeeze into the slot. After a stint of walking the slot canyon, which involves a couple of minor down climbs, Wire Pass opens into a large amphitheater and meets Buckskin Gulch. Here,

Paria Canyon

chipped low on the right wall, you'll find petroglyphs of bighorn sheep.

At the other side of the amphitheater, the trail comes to a T-junction. Head to the right down Buckskin Gulch. Approximately 6.5 miles in you'll run across the first pools of water. These pools generally last for a mile and a half and are most often stagnant and very cold. Buckskin veterans refer to the largest of the pools as The Cesspool because of its stagnant, smelly nature.

After you leave the last pool of water, the canyon walls drop to about 100 feet and Middle Trail becomes accessible. If the weather is threatening, Middle Trail is the only emergency route to scramble up and out. The route is difficult to pinpoint, but if you're lucky you'll spot two bighorn sheep petroglyphs about 20 feet up a rock on the left side of the Gulch. The route evidently starts just to the left of these petroglyphs. Some hikers climb out of the Gulch on this trail to set up camp on the slickrock rim their first night. After Middle Trail there is usually no deep wading.

A mile or so before the Paria River confluence you'll hit the rock jam. This jam has boulders the size of large vehicles and requires a fun descent and belly crawl to get through. This is the most serious obstacle in the Gulch. A 30-foot rope is useful for lowering packs and group members down. The rock jam includes boulders and masses of driftwood washed into piles by the flash floods that tear through the Gulch. These rats' nests of debris are sometimes stuck above your head where the slot narrows or are found in side indentations in the walls. Here at the rock jam, they fill in crevices throughout the site. Below the jam are a handful of seeps where fresh water can sometimes be had.

There are a number of camping options for your first night. As mentioned above, exiting at Middle Trail is one option (if you can locate it). Finding a relatively safe ledge when there is *no* chance of flash flooding is another. But the most often used option is to find a level area of grass and trees on a river bend about a half mile before the confluence with the Paria. If these campsites are full, continue to the confluence and go south on the Paria for less than a mile to more campsites.

My group ended up making camp in the Gulch on a high sandbar at a wide spot in the canyon. Though it was not the safest place to camp, our choices were limited because it was already dark (remember to get an early start). We named our sandbar Club Med because of the wonderful greenery around it and the respite it provided after a day of hiking and wading pools, which were thigh high on this April trip.

DAY 2: The second day is spent primarily in the Paria Narrows. At the confluence, turn north (left) and head up into the narrows of the Paria River. This section requires a lot of river walking, so sandals or water shoes are appropriate. The headwaters of the Paria come from snowmelt at Bryce Canyon, so the water levels depend on the year's precipitation. The narrows in the Paria are more open than those in the Buckskin, and the colors and heights change as you make your way up and out to more open desert.

About 0.75 mile up the Paria you come to Slide Arch, which is really just a large piece of rock that has fallen in the position of an arch. Continue following the river and wash 7.25 miles toward White House Campground. The exit spot is marked with a brown BLM sign that directs you up and out of the wash on the right.

While hiking up the Paria you'll come across some really beautiful Creamsicle walls that are huecoed at the base and look like something out of *The Lord of the Rings*. This section of the trail can be a drier and hotter slog than the magnificent Buckskin, but it is lovely in its own way. When water is running, you'll have a great way to keep cool.

RESOURCES

SHUTTLE INFORMATION

Paria Outpost & Outfitters: 928-691-1047; www.paria.com; pariaoutpost@yahoo.com; nearest shuttle to trailheads

End of the Trail Shuttles (Betty Price): 928-355-2252; near Lee's Ferry

Catalina Martinez: 928-355-2295; near Lee's Ferry

USEFUL WEB SITES AND PHONE NUMBERS

BLM Paria permit access: www.az.blm.gov/paria; check a calendar for permit availability and make reservations

BLM Kanab field office: 435-644-4600

A LITTLE HISTORY, GEOLOGY, FLORA, AND FAUNA

In 1984 the Lower Paria and Vermillion Cliffs were designated as wilderness area. In 2000 the area was designated by President Clinton as the Vermillion Cliffs National Monument, currently managed by the BLM. Strangely enough, the trailheads for this area are actually within the Escalante Staircase National Monument, but once on the trail you enter the BLM Kanab Field Office Resource Area.

The natural beauty of these slot canyons is the force that continually pulls outdoor-lovers to the area. Geologic formations like the Cockscomb, Buckskin Mountain, Buckskin Gulch, and the candy-cane-stripe cliffs that line the roads give the national monuments their appeal. As you drive from White House Campground to the Wire Pass Trailhead, you'll notice the colorful eye-catching cliffs next to the road. At mile marker 24 the cliffs begin to rise from the ground at an angle, becoming a red, wrinkled, chunky formation known as the Cockscomb. Wire Pass Trailhead is found in the Cockscomb, but as you drop into Buckskin Gulch you are really following a geologic trail back in time, worn through Buckskin Mountain.

Juniper, cheatgrass, sage, and yellow rose thrive in the desert country and rock cracks outside the Gulch. In the Gulch itself plant life has less opportunity to flourish. At wet times of year, intermittent cottonwoods in the Gulch provide a stark, green, lush contrast to the rock walls and smaller plants. Though visible in many areas where the walls open up, for the most part they haven't been able to withstand flash floods that can reach 20 to 30 feet high.

These floods bring seeds from the upper desert floor that take root within the Gulch until washed out by the next flood. Above the flash flood line, hanging gardens provide an almost landscaped atmosphere. Along the Paria, tamarisk and willows grow and flood out again in an endless cycle. Life in the stagnant pools of water in the Gulch centers around bacteria decomposing organic matter, which can include plants, logs, and sometimes dead animals.

Birds glide along the cliffs where they open up, and a mouse or two sometimes runs the corridors with canyoneers. I have often hiked in the

Buckskin to the sound of raven wings beating the air. They swoop around open bends of the cliff walls and down the corridor as if the canyon were an interstate. A variety of birds can be heard singing throughout the late-morning hours.

Also in the area is the Paria Movie Set and Ghost Town, located along US 89 toward Kanab. *The Outlaw Josie Wales* with Clint Eastwood was filmed here. Tourists often stop to peruse this site.

The Paria Outpost sits between the starting and ending trailheads and boasts what it claims to be the "best barbeque west of the Mississippi." On Friday and Saturday nights they offer a buffet and usually have live music. No other restaurants are available in the area. Page, Arizona, is 30 miles to the west and Kanab is 43 miles east. Fill up with gas and supplies before entering the area from either direction. The two trailheads, the Outpost, and the ranger station are practically all you'll find along US 89 in this area.

Petroglyph panel

Grand Staircase–Escalante National Monument

🥾 COYOTE GULCH

A Hidden Desert Tributary of Life

On September 18, 1996, to the surprise and consternation of many Utahans, President Bill Clinton declared that 1.7 million acres of public land in Garfield and Kane Counties would be set aside as a national monument, now known as Grand Staircase–Escalante National Monument. This is not a place of stairs or escalators; it is a

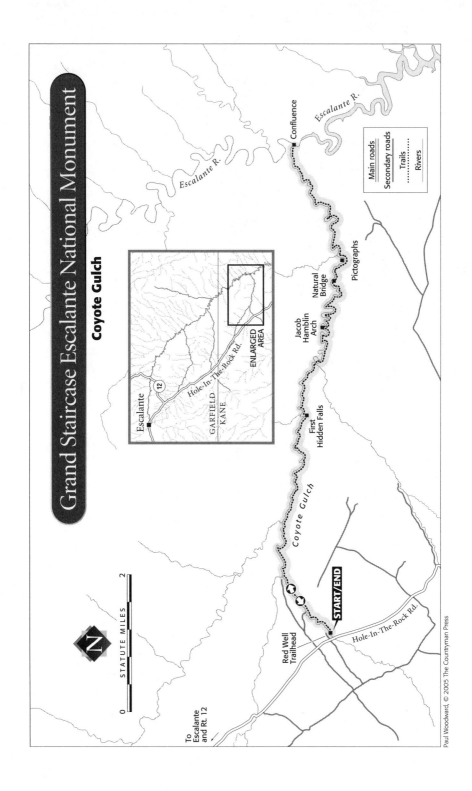

Grand Staircase Escalante National Monument

Coyote Gulch

Jacob Hamblin Arch

land with strata revealing a staircase of 200 million years of geographic journaling.

Virtually untouched for hundreds of years, it holds undisturbed remains of the Ancestral Puebloans: granaries, pictographs, petroglyphs, and tools that expose much about their civilization. Escalante is a rough area of mostly unimproved roads that are impassable at times. Entry into

Hiking Coyote Gulch

this land of soaring colorful cliffs, plateaus, mesas, buttes, pinnacles, and canyons is a bit more than just a walk in the park. This is a land of real adventuring.

Coyote Gulch is the most popular hiking destination in the Escalante Canyons, and justifiably so. Soaring red cliffs tower above a ribbon of water, rich with strands of green in the form of trees, willows, grasses, and flowers. The stream is a product of underground seepages and springs. It flows into the Escalante River 13 miles down canyon, where the Gulch ends.

Highlights of the trip include two arches, a natural bridge, dripping springs, and several waterfalls. Each day is a delight as you hike below gorgeous red canyon walls. Despite its popularity, this is a wonderful wilderness retreat.

Because of the remote nature of the Grand Staircase–Escalante National Monument, the approach is not easy. You'll have to drive 30 to 35 miles on a rutted washboard road to get to the trailhead. Low-clearance cars make the trek out every weekend, but you'll be more comfortable in a four-wheel-drive vehicle.

SPORT: Backpacking, backcountry camping

RATING: The terrain in Coyote Gulch is relatively flat, with little to no elevation change except for the first drop down into the Gulch. Trudging through the sand can become difficult and will give your legs a good workout.

DISTANCE: 26 miles round trip

TIME: Four days is plenty of time to fully explore the Gulch if you cover 6 to 6.5 miles a day at a good pace. This gives you two days in and two days out. Depending on your stamina and backpacking experience, you can shorten the trip to two or three days. Just keep in mind that if you cut it too close on time, you may have to head back without visiting the best parts of the Gulch. The trail gets better the farther in you go and all of the primary arches, waterfalls, and bridges are found within the last 7 miles of the trail, so plan adequate time if you wish to experience the full wonder of Coyote Gulch.

GETTING THERE: Grand Staircase–Escalante National Monument is located in the south-central portion of the state. Final access to the monument is via UT 12, a scenic byway. There are a number of possible routes to UT 12, and the one listed here includes two more scenic byways. From Salt Lake City, head south on I-15. Just past Cove Fort, after approximately 168 miles, take Exit 132 toward I-70 East. Follow I-70 for 23 miles to Exit 23 and then head south on US 89 for 65 miles before heading east on UT 12.

Highway 12 takes you through the town of Escalante and connects with Escalante State Park, the Grand Staircase National Monument, and its visitors' center. Travel time from Salt Lake City is about five hours (a total of 314 miles).

Once in Escalante, continue along UT 12 for 6 miles to Hole-in-the-Rock Road. Signage for the road is ample, and it heads off to the right. Follow this road for 30 miles to the Red Well Trailhead. A small sign marks the turnoff. Proceed another 1.5 miles to the trailhead. The 30-odd-mile stretch took us one hour and 45 minutes in a car because of the washboard ruts.

TRAIL: A number of trailheads lead into Coyote Gulch. Here I'll focus on Red Well because you drop into the Gulch rather quickly and have less cross-desert travel time. The length of this trip also creates a pleasant backpacking experience, with full exposure to the Gulch.

Coyote Gulch is pure backcountry. Always pay attention to landmarks, because once you leave the trailhead sign-in box the only markers along the trail are occasional cairns. The good news is that the trail is well worn and primarily follows a wash. Just remember to keep your bearings and use the landmarks. GPS coordinates will help you pinpoint specific sites, but once you hit the stream you simply follow it to the confluence with the Escalante River.

The trail is a combination of sandy riverbed, packed trail, and wet stream crossings. The water is seldom more than ankle deep, but you cross it often. You can't help but get wet. I have hiked it in both sandals and boots, but I prefer boots because the sandals don't provide much support on the sandy sections of trail. I've seen other hikers do it in sandals, and even bare feet. The water is deepest during spring runoff in late April and May. Keep an eye on the trail and the main streambed. I've found that though there is always a trail to follow, sometimes it wanders up a side canyon, up a tributary feeding into the main gulch, or simply off at an angle. When in doubt, always stick to the primary stream.

Archaeological and historic sites are fragile, non-renewable resources. Do not touch rock art or climb in ruins. Leave everything as you find it. Collecting artifacts is prohibited. Services and water are not available in the Monument. When heading into the backcountry make sure you have a permit and that others know your plans. Don't travel or hike alone.

All roads within the Monument's interior, except portions of the Burr Trail and Johnson Canyon Road, are unimproved. Most roads are dirt or gravel and can get rough and rocky. Some roads traverse areas of deep sand and require high clearance or four-wheel drive. Gasoline is available in the communities surrounding the Monument, but not within. Be prepared so that adventure doesn't turn to disaster.

OPTIONAL DAY HIKE: The Calf Creek Trail is a desert oasis managed by the BLM. Well marked, it runs beside Calf Creek, so called because pioneers once used the box canyon area to keep weaned calves in the natural pasture. One of the best-known trails in the Grand Staircase–Escalante National Monument, the hike ends at a 126-foot waterfall that cascades down a reddish-brown face covered with Christmas green moss. The falls collect in a large pool at the base. Water flows year-round, coming from large seeps and springs, helping animals and plant life to thrive.

The trip to Lower Calf Creek Falls takes three hours for the average hiker to complete and covers 5.4 miles round trip. Make a day of it by taking along a picnic for lunch and your bathing suits for a swim in the pool beneath the waterfall. The BLM provides a written guide at the trailhead that points out areas of interest along the trail, including well-preserved petroglyphs, beaver dams, and other flora and fauna. White and pink Navajo sandstone surrounds the trail and much of the path is covered with this sand.

We began this hike in late afternoon and made it back just before dark, taking time to watch an illegal rapeller descend the waterfall. Because of our late start we didn't have time to take a swim, and the April evening was a bit chilly anyway. But if you're hiking in the heat of the day, a quick dip will cool you off.

To reach the trailhead, drive east from the visitors' center in Escalante toward Boulder on UT 12 for 16.3 miles to the Calf Creek

Campground. The trail is located at the back of the campground, less than a half mile from the highway.

MAXIMUM GROUP SIZE: Regulations allow 12 people per backcountry permit.

CAMPING: In Coyote Gulch all backcountry camping is free but requires a permit. A couple of backcountry toilets are set up in the Gulch (GPS coordinates: UTM 12 S 0496330/4141449 and UTM 12 S 0496320/4141519).

If you wish to day-hike and car camp before heading out into the backcountry, the campground at Escalante State Park comes complete with nice showers, modern bathroom facilities, and Wide Hollow Reservoir, which offers canoeing, fishing, or motorboating. Canoes are available to rent for $5 an hour, $10 for four hours, or $20 for the day, and life vests and paddles are included. Reservations can be made by calling 1-800-322-3770. Campsites at the state park run $14 per night. If you make a reservation you'll be charged an additional $7 reservation fee, for a total of $21. Firewood is $3 an armload or you can bring in your own. The Escalante State Park campground is also the access point for the Petrified Forest Trail.

Another popular camping area is the Calf Creek Campground, but no reservations are allowed and it fills quickly. Campsites are only $7 per night, but you must haul out your garbage because no trash bins or collection is available. This campground is also the trailhead for the popular Calf Creek Falls day hike.

SEASON: Spring and fall are the most popular and pleasant times on the trail, though there are occasional rainstorms in the spring. If you're in the Gulch during a heavy rainstorm you'll be afforded the great pleasure of watching the waterfalls cascade from the cliff walls. Summer temperatures reach 90 to 100 degrees Fahrenheit, and the arid windy heat makes June, July, and August a miserable time to haul a pack in the desert.

Flash floods are possible at any time of year, but the rainy season lasts from July through September. If you're looking for seclusion, it's worth noting that fewer people visit in September and October than during the spring. In flash flood season hikers must camp on high ground and watch for storm alerts.

PERMITS: A permit is required but is currently free and can be secured at the visitors' center upon arrival. Visitors' center hours are 7:45 AM–4:30 PM.

FEES: No fees are required to hike in Coyote Gulch.

CLOTHING AND EQUIPMENT: Spring and fall temperatures fluctuate between cold and comfortable. Because of this, I recommend hiking with light layers that can be added or removed as needed. During the heat of summer, lightweight clothing, sunscreen, and a hat are all musts, but be prepared for cold nights. Bug spray is necessary to keep the mosquitoes and deer flies at bay after the hatch (usually May). Bring a pair of sandals as well as hiking boots. Sandals give your feet a breather after a day in the boot, and come in handy for streams and waterfalls. In winter, desert areas can be covered in a light blanket of snow and dirt roads may be impassable. Visitation is low at this time.

No fires are allowed while backcountry camping so bring a headlamp or flashlight. Aside from the usual camping and packing supplies, you'll also need a camp stove if you intend to cook. Bring a rope to string food up in a tree, which will keep rodents from chewing through your tent and backpack.

Backcountry camping regulations require that you haul out your own trash. This includes all toilet paper. Bring bags for this purpose. Fortunately, Coyote Gulch follows a stream so you won't have to pack in all your water, although you'll need a good purifier. The visitors' center can supply free maps for the areas around Escalante, so there is no need to secure those ahead of time. A tent and sleeping pad are good ideas, too. We woke up one morning to find a baby scorpion keeping itself warm beneath our sleeping bags.

SUGGESTED ITINERARY

DAY 1: Secure your permit from the Escalante National Monument Visitors' Center. Follow Hole-in-the-Rock Road to the Red Well Trailhead. Park, sign in on the register, and strap on your pack and head to the right on the old red-sand road. At 0.57 mile the trail descends into a dry wash that you follow down into the Gulch. Depending on the time of year, water will start to appear between 0.9 and 1.5 miles. Once you reach water, the trees, rabbitbrush, weeds, and flowers transform the dry brown desert into a green oasis.

Approximately 2 miles in you come across the first slot falls (UTM 12 S 0490848/4142361), although they are difficult to see. You can hear them, but to get a look at them you'll have to top a sand hill—the first of the Gulch. When you drop down the other side you'll see a mucky iridescent pool of water in front of a small slot canyon to the right. You must remove your boots and squeeze into this slot, which is just large enough to walk through, and then follow it back through successive pools to find the four curvaceous red rock levels down which the water cascades.

When you're ready to leave you'll see more than one trail. Head to the far side of the mucky pool and follow the trail over the red mound of sand. In April the water is warm and the pools are full of tadpoles, frog eggs, and water skeeters. It's a great resting spot.

While the Gulch starts with some pretty unimpressive scenery, after a few miles towering red walls appear reaching so far into the sky you can get drunk on their height. A new one seems to loom at every turn. At 8 miles you come to Jacob Hamblin Arch, the first of a number of absolutely magnificent desert arches and bridges that make the trek through Coyote Gulch worth every step. From here the scenery becomes ever more inspiring.

Make camp under the massive waves of cliffs, and enjoy a night of stargazing far from any man-made light.

DAY 2: The last part of the trail is filled with the arches and waterfalls for which Coyote Gulch is famous. At mile 9 you reach Coyote Natural Bridge, an arch formed by water. A set of large red and white pictographs can be found approximately 0.5 mile past the natural bridge (UTM 12 S 0498071/4140879). They are up on the cliff face off the left side of the trail. A number of trails lead up the mountain to the cliff, and you must climb one of these to see the pictographs up close.

Cliff Arch is 10.5 miles in, and at mile 11 you hike across one of several waterfalls. The trail ends at the stream's junction with the Escalante River. If you are squeezing the trip into three days you may want to hike back to Jacob Hamlin Arch today. (If you are definitely doing the three-day version and will be returning to the Jacob Hamblin Arch area to camp a second night, there is no reason to carry your backpack on the second day. Just day-hike down to the Escalante on day 2.)

I have camped near the stream and towering walls, the sounds of water resonating through the night. It sounds as though the stream is running quietly right next to the tent, although it's really the echo of the river 30 feet away.

DAYS 3 AND 4: Backtrack down the trail, enjoying a second view of all the wonders Coyote Gulch has to offer.

RESOURCES

USEFUL WEB SITES AND PHONE NUMBERS
Camping reservations at state parks: 1-800-322-3770, 8 AM–5 PM Monday–Friday; www.ut.blm.gov/monument
Escalante Interagency Visitors' Center: 435-826-5499

TOURS AND GUIDES
View a list of licensed outfitters in the area at www.ut.blm.gov/monument.

A LITTLE HISTORY, GEOLOGY, FLORA, AND FAUNA

In the 1880s geologist Clarence Dutton described the high plateaus of southern Utah and northern Arizona as being "like a great stairway." The staircase of Escalante extends 150 miles from bottom to top, rises 3,500 feet in elevation, and represents nearly 260 million years of geologic history. As each layer of sediment was deposited it preserved evidence of the oceans, sand dunes, coal swamps, and the streams and rivers that meandered across the land through the ages.

Each layer, whether sandstone, siltstone, mudstone, or limestone, records in rock the record of the past. As the Colorado Plateau slowly began to rise, it formed the cliffs and canyons of Escalante. The layers are named according to their color: Chocolate, Vermillion, White, Gray, and Pink. The first layer was laid in a warm ocean environment. Each consecutive layer reveals the past in a three-dimensional history book. One of the best places to view the Grand Staircase is from US 89 between Kanab and the Paria River.

The Monument is a treasure chest of history, with countless petrified shells, bones, leaves, wood, teeth, tracks, and subtropic vegetation fossils. Like the rocks, the fossils tell a story of the environmental changes and animal life millions of years ago. Scientists are especially interested in the rocks formed between 75 and 94 million years ago in the Cretaceous period of the Mesozoic era. This section of rock is a yellow band found three or four layers down from the cliff top.

Studies of the formations within the Monument have yielded more information about North America in the time not long before the dinosaurs vanished than any other place on the continent. Fossils of many new species of marine reptiles, dinosaurs, small mammals, birds, lizards, giant crocodiles, turtles, amphibians, plants, and invertebrates have been found here. Thanks to the vast store of remains and the exposed rock formations that make them accessible, this area is a haven for paleontologists and historians.

Escalante was named after two Spanish priests, Fathers Dominguez and Escalante, who led an exploration party through the Southwest in

1776. In 1886 the first European settlers to the area officially named the town of Escalante.

Hole-in-the-Rock was named for a Mormon expedition, which traveled the Hole-in-the-Rock Road in 1879. They lowered their 83 wagons 2,000 feet down through a hole in the rock wall and ferried them across the Colorado River to establish a Mormon settlement in southern Utah.

Because Escalante was one of the last frontiers to be explored, and due to the harsh environment, many of the animals in the area are much as they were in pioneer times. Efforts are ongoing to reintroduce animals that have been forced out of the area. Biologists at the Monument have successfully reintroduced desert bighorn sheep and pronghorn to their historic habitat on the open plains of Escalante, and there are plans to bring river otters back to the Escalante River.

I've heard the swish of lizards through the grass at every turn while hiking Coyote Gulch. Different sizes and colors, it seems that no two are alike. The biologist at Monument headquarters informed me that the sagebrush lizard and great basin collared lizard are the types most often seen along the trail.

During spring and fall, Escalante is a stopover for migrating birds like sparrow and finch that are making their way to and from Central America. In addition, there are a large number of raptors in the area. Golden eagles are year-round residents, and ravens, peregrine, and red-tailed hawks make Escalante their home as well. They prey on the many mice that you'll hear rattling the leaves as you hike. I once came upon a soft grassy knoll situated about 50 feet above my head at the base of a massive red cliff. Halfway up the sheer face sat a huge eagle's nest, its tan, dead grasses a stark contrast to the red stone face.

Always shake out shoes and clothes in the morning before dressing, as scorpions find their way into various crevices. Beware of rattlesnakes and watch where you put your hands when climbing. Poison ivy grows near water sources in the Gulch, so know how to identify it (leaves in threes) and then stay away.

On our last trip we saw frogs in all stages of maturation: adult, tadpole, eggs. Remember that all animals, plants, and minerals in the park are protected. Treat them all with respect. In the sparse desert, life has always come to the streams and rivers; it is the only way to survive. You walk where the coyote and fox, the pronghorn and burrowing owl, and generations of previous civilizations have walked before you. You become part of the history of these places that have given us life. Walk carefully and listen to the wind and the echoes of your own voice.

Capitol Reef National Park

Capitol Reef National Park

🚶 UPPER MULEY TWIST TRAIL

One Vantage Point, Two Completely Different Views

Ranger Ben has us sitting at the foot of a Fremont Indian petroglyph panel just down the road from the Capitol Reef Visitors' Center. We're talking about the Fremont River Valley and what life was like for the prehistoric Native Americans that lived here and then suddenly disappeared around A.D. 1300. He passes around shards of pottery and photocopies of moccasins found, along with small cobs of maize and woven basket fibers. The Hopi believed the Grand Canyon was the birthplace of Man. As Man emerged the gods told the people to head in

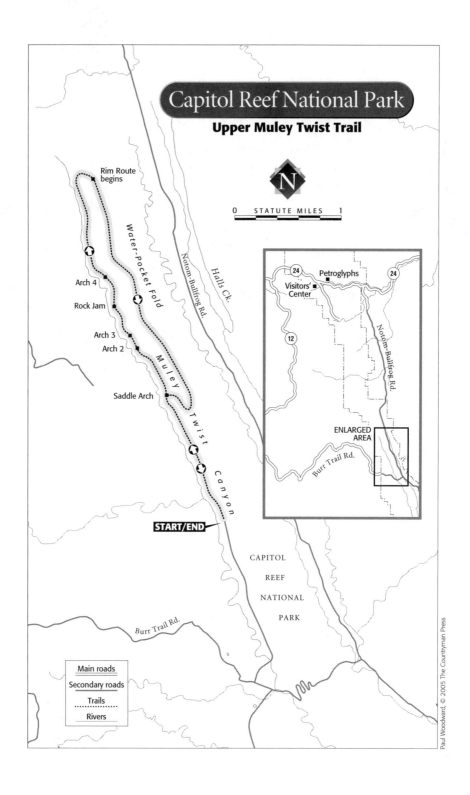

Capitol Reef National Park

Upper Muley Twist Trail

N

0   STATUTE MILES   1

Rim Route
begins

Water-pocket Fold

Halls Ck.

Notom-Bullfrog Rd.

Arch 4

Rock Jam

Arch 3

Arch 2

Saddle Arch

Muley

Twist

Canyon

START/END

Petroglyphs
24
Visitors'
Center
24

12

Notom-Bullfrog Rd.

ENLARGED
AREA

Burr Trail Rd.

CAPITOL

REEF

NATIONAL

PARK

Burr Trail Rd.

Main roads
Secondary roads
Trails
Rivers

Paul Woodward, © 2005 The Countryman Press

View from the top of Upper Muley Twist Trail

the four cardinal directions: north, south, east, and west. The Fremont people were those who headed north.

Besides amazing scenery, one of the richest parts of Capitol Reef National Park is its history. When adventuring in this area you are immersed in the past, including the remains of ancient Native American cultures and more recent Mormon settlements. Washes, slot canyons, trails, and of course the orchards and fruit for which the park is famous make for a very full and interesting national park adventure.

This weekend adventure includes the most scenic and geologically rich routes in the park: Upper Muley Twist Canyon and a day hike to a stunning and accessible 133-foot-wide red rock bridge on the Hickman Bridge Trail. It includes a dip in a Fremont River waterfall and evening relaxation in a lush riverside park lined with red cliffs inhabited by mule deer and marmot.

SPORT: Backpacking, hiking, camping

RATING: Upper Muley Twist Canyon, moderate to strenuous; Hickman Bridge Trail, easy

DISTANCE: Upper Muley Twist Canyon, 9.6-mile loop; Hickman Bridge Trail, 2 miles round trip

TIME: Two days to backpack Upper Muley Twist Canyon or one long day hike (approximately eight hours, including time for lunch and day hikes in the area).

GETTING THERE: Capitol Reef National Park is located in south-central Utah. From Salt Lake City, take I-15 south to Nephi, and then pick up UT 28 south to Salina. Get on I-70 for a few miles, and then take the Sigurd exit to UT 24, which takes you to Capitol Reef in about 80 miles. Total distance from Salt Lake City is 225 miles. Plan on a four-hour drive.

Drive east for 9 miles on UT 24 from Capitol Reef National Park Visitors' Center to Upper Muley Twist Canyon. Take in the wonderful scenery and geologic wonders of the area as you drive through. Look for a paved road on the right that leads to Notom. Turn here and drive 33 miles south to the junction with the Burr Trail Road. You'll pass Cedar Mesa Campground on the way, a primitive camping area where you may choose to stay when you've finished the Upper Muley Twist Trail.

Turn onto Burr Trail Road, which takes you to the Burr Trail switchbacks, a highlight of the trip. Beautiful, dramatic auburn cliffs usher you up onto the Waterpocket Fold, a 100-mile wrinkle of sandstone in the earth's crust. The switchbacks gain elevation very quickly. After 3.2 miles on the Burr Trail you'll see a small sign on the right marking the dirt road to Upper Muley Twist Canyon. Turn right and after 0.4 mile you'll see a trail register and another sign advising you that to continue on you will need a four-wheel-drive vehicle. The trailhead is another 2.4 miles down this road. If you don't have a high-clearance vehicle, you'll have to park here and walk to the trailhead.

▐▌ TRAIL: Upper Muley Twist Canyon is a strenuous but amazing trail. The canyon cuts directly down the spine of the Waterpocket Fold, revealing astounding views of the Wingate red rock on one side, with its impressive arches and unusual forms, and the geological wonders of the Waterpocket Fold and Strike Valley on the other. When you reach the Rim Route on top of the Fold, the views become unparalleled.

The trail starts in a wash (UTM 12 S 0495887/4192694; elevation 5,879), with the deep red Wingate sandstone formation rising on both sides. The trail has no official markings, but you can leave your vehicle at the Strike Valley Overlook parking area and just follow the wash north. Another trail at the parking area leads to the Strike Valley Overlook, but this isn't your trail.

As you head up the wash, you'll occasionally see runoff washes entering the main riverbed. Stay to the right. At 1.6 miles you come to Saddle Arch (UTM 12 S 0494763/4194892; elevation 5,914), the first arch on the trail. It's the only named arch on the route. Not far down the trail you'll see a sign marking the Rim Route. You won't be joining the Rim Trail until you get farther up Muley Twist, but this is where you'll drop back into the canyon to complete the loop.

Continue up the wash another 1.3 miles, and look high to your left for the second arch (UTM 12 494263 E/4195671 N). The third arch is only 753 feet past the second (UTM 12 494127 E/4195856 N). Farther up the trail, between the third and fourth arches, you'll run into a set of huge boulders blocking the wash. Bypass them on either side. The fourth and last arch is 0.8 mile up canyon from the previous one, and it sits at the bottom of a slot canyon that enters the main wash on the left. (UTM 12 S 0493545/4197038; elevation 6,099) You can hike right up to it.

Shortly after this final arch, cairns lead you up and out of the streambed to avoid obstacles in the wash. The trail to this upper shelf, though strenuous and often steep, takes you about 100 feet above the wash for a little over a half mile before dropping back down.

Hiking the Hickman Bridge Trail

You have covered half the trail at this point. If you've backpacked in and plan to stay the night you may want to consider looking for a campsite before heading out of the canyon, as there are not many choices once you hit the rim. I've found camping spots on the rim that were flat enough for tent placement, but most included large anthills.

Not far from this point, the canyon narrows and dead-ends. Climb up a small hill to the left. From here on you'll need to watch closely for cairns marking the way. If you go more than 25 yards without seeing one you should reevaluate your position. The cairns lead you to the Rim Trail (marked with a sign), where you leave the canyon.

The ascent is full of switchbacks, exposed Class 4 ledges, and dramatic scenery. Hike carefully to avoid falling. After a 200-foot elevation gain you'll suddenly find yourself on top of the Waterpocket Fold at an altitude of 6,670 feet. The views before you include part of the Strike Valley and the Waterpocket Fold on one side, and the slickrock Wingate Formation you just passed through on the other. Over the next 2 miles of trail you'll see all the arches you viewed on the way in, only from a higher vantage point. You are mostly traveling up and down white slickrock and following cairns through this stretch, with top-of-the-world views in every direction.

You soon come to a small sign marked CANYON ROUTE. From here the trail drops back into the canyon, where you complete the loop by reentering the wash near Saddle Arch. Finish by simply making your way back to your vehicle at the trailhead.

Note: Upper Muley Twist Trail is not appropriate for most children because of its length and exposure. There are a number of day hikes that would be considered child-friendly, including Hickman Bridge Trail, but backcountry exploring in the harsh Utah desert is not child's play.

OPTIONAL ACTIVITIES: Cathedral Valley, the northern backcountry section of Capitol Reef National Park, has a 60-mile loop that makes for a strenuous multi-day mountain biking trek through red Entrada sandstone monoliths that reach 500 feet high—cathedrals of the Southwest. It's best to do the route with a support vehicle, as elevations vary as much as 2,140 feet. Be sure to alert park rangers to your plans and secure the necessary backcountry permits.

Start at River Ford off UT 24. If you primarily want to ride downhill, head out on the western leg of the loop, camping at Cathedral Valley Campground and finishing on Caineville Wash Road.

MAXIMUM GROUP SIZE: If you are camping in the backcountry, your group size must not exceed 12 people.

CAMPING: On the trail, all camping is backcountry. Choose your own spot. Practice a Leave No Trace camping ethic. Pack everything out, including toilet paper.

In the national park there are three campgrounds: Cathedral, Cedar Mesa, and Fruita. Cathedral Campground is located in the northern section of the park, while Cedar Mesa is in the central region. Both are primitive and have no water. There are six sites at each campground with picnic tables, fire pits, pit toilets, and grills. No fees are charged, but it is first come, first served.

Fruita Campground is considered the park's main campground. Located just up the road from the visitors' center, it has flush toilets, tables, dumpsites, and grills (no showers). Seventy-one sites are available with seven tent-only sites. No reservations are available, and during peak season the campground fills by noon. The rangers recommend arriving by 10 AM if you want to secure a site. Peak season runs Easter to Labor Day. There is also a group campsite that can be reserved well in advance if you have a party of at least 40. For more information on group site reservations, call 435-425-3791, ext. 160.

SEASON: Spring and fall are prime time; summer is very hot and winter is cold and quite snowy.

PERMITS: The National Park Service requires backcountry permits for anyone camping in the backcountry. There is currently no charge for permits, and they can be picked up at the visitors' center when you arrive.

FEES: No fees.

CLOTHING AND EQUIPMENT: The weather is unpredictable in spring and fall. Dress in layers so you can adjust as the day warms. Always take a rain jacket, just in case. I recommend two pairs of shoes: good hiking boots and water sandals. The sandals provide a great break for your feet at the end of the day.

Binoculars are fun for getting a closer look at arches, but not necessary. Bring sunglasses, sunscreen, lip balm, and a camera, and make sure you have a gallon of water per person, per day. There is no water available on the Hickman Bridge day hike or on the Upper Muley Twist Trail.

The National Park Service suggests a topographic map for Upper Muley Twist Canyon (UMTC), but I found that a compass, directions, and the cairns were sufficient.

SUGGESTED ITINERARY

DAY 1: Arrive at Capitol Reef National Park Visitors' Center and learn about the area. There is a short Capitol Reef introduction video, and maps and trail information are available. If you intend to camp on the UMTC Trail, get your backcountry permit here.

There are 15 day hikes located along UT 24, but I recommend starting with the Hickman Bridge Trail as a warm-up. Located 2 miles east of the visitors' center, it is easily accessible and rivals any arch in the state. The hike to Hickman Arch is moderate and self-guided, with a trail guide and markers that outline points of interest and introduce you to some of the geology and flora of the area.

The hiking trail to this bridge offers scenic, not-to-be-missed views. Along the way you'll see a Fremont Indian pit house and a granary. Once you reach the bridge, which is completely accessible on foot, you can continue along a trail to an overview of Fruita and the orchards below. This is one of the most popular hiking trails in the park, but it's worth visiting nevertheless. The Fremont Culture Walk is found along the same road. It consists of a short boardwalk at the base of a panel of petroglyphs. It's a good stop for anyone interested in Indian cultural remains.

For dinner, return to the scenic drive that starts at the visitors' center and follow it a few blocks to a park. Picnic tables, potable water, and fire pits are available. The park is watered often and stays a beautiful lush green all through the summer. You can sit at the feet of dark orange cliffs while watching mule deer nibble their way through the grass and riverside foliage.

I once rested quietly against a tree near the river while deer picked their way closer and closer, at times getting within 15 feet. They are wild things grown less timid by their exposure to humans, but still beautiful, feral creatures. At dusk the marmots pop out of holes and travel the hillsides and picnic spots on the other side of the road.

Retire to the campsite of your choice. If you have problems securing a site, you can camp on nearby BLM land or get a back-country permit for any nights you wish to spend in an undeveloped campground. In the backcountry, you must set up camp at least a half mile from roads and trailheads. Camp out of sight (and sound) of the trail and other campers, and camp away from flowing water and archaeological and historic sites and junctions.

DAY 2: Head to Upper Muley Twist Canyon. Start early if you decide to do the entire trail in one day, as you have six to eight hours of walking ahead of you. If you make it a two-day trip, plan for around four hours of hiking with plenty of time to rest up.

Remember that no fires are allowed in the backcountry. You must pack out all trash, including food scraps and toilet paper. Pets are not permitted on trails or in the backcountry, and collecting items of any type is prohibited.

If you're not staying in the backcountry, Cedar Mesa Campground is nearby.

DAY 3: If you're staying on the Upper Muley Twist Trail for an extra day, you can spend it finishing the hike before heading back down UT 24 for a stop at the Fremont River waterfall. Take a cool dip in the falls and then start the drive home.

If you did the UMTC Trail in one day and are looking for more adventure on day three, there are a number of slot canyons that widen into washes along the Burr Trail. Burro Wash, Cottonwood Wash, and Sheets Gulch are all found on the way to the Upper Muley Trail. Choose just one to explore, as each represents a day-long adventure.

RESOURCES

TOURS AND GUIDES
Hondoo Rivers and Trails: 1-800-322-2696; www.hondoo.com
Wild Hare Expeditions: 1-888-304-4273; www.color-country.net/~thehare

FOUR-WHEEL-DRIVE RENTALS
ATV Rentals and Tours: 435-425-3345, full and half-day rentals
Capitol Reef Backcountry Outfitters: 1-866-747-3972
High Country Tours: 435-836-2047

USEFUL WEB SITES AND PHONE NUMBERS
Capitol Reef Area: www.capitolreef.org
National Park Service: www.nps.gov/care
Capitol Reef National Park: 435-425-3791

A LITTLE HISTORY, GEOLOGY, FLORA, AND FAUNA

Capitol Reef is characterized by a 100-mile-long bulge in the earth's crust, the Waterpocket Fold. The fold has been sculpted and weathered over time into today's wonderland of canyons, domes, and arches. Sometime during the Cretaceous Period, over 65 million years ago, the sedimentary rocks in the Capitol Reef area were subjected to such intense pressure by the subduction of one tectonic plate moving by another that the pressure caused a giant wrinkle called a monocline uplift.

An enormous basin that had collected ocean and river sediment for eons was lifted and folded to reveal a history of ancient seas and deserts representing millions of years of geological creation. This monocline has been a formidable barrier to east-west travel. It was named Capitol Reef by early explorers, many of whom were seamen who termed all barriers as reefs. The first part of the name comes from the massive white domes found across the park, which are reminiscent of the Capitol building in Washington, D.C.

The Fremont River and its tributaries run amid these domes, monoclines, arches, and towering walls. The availability of water has been the attraction for settlers throughout the valley's history. Some archeologists estimate that Indian civilizations have called the area home for over 12,000 years, and more recent history involves Mormon pioneers, government explorers, and prospectors. Petroglyphs, granaries, and other Indian remains tell us pieces of the Native American story along the banks of the Fremont River. Hundreds of sites have been identified, from lithic scatters to caves and rock art panels. Many are world renowned, while others are visited primarily by the scientific community.

When modern pioneers moved into the area in the 1870s, they found abundant proof of prehistoric occupation. Eph Hanks, a polygamist seeking to evade arrest by hiding in this remote region, made the Fremont River valley his home. He was responsible for planting the first two hundred fruit trees in the area. Others followed suit. When residents sought to establish a post office they chose the name Fruita to honor their excellent orchards and vineyards.

Today these orchards are preserved as a Rural Historic Landscape. The orchards are composed of approximately 2,700 cherry, apricot, pear, apple, peach, plum, mulberry, almond, and walnut trees. The National Park Service maintains the orchards year-round and visitors are given the opportunity to taste and buy in-season fruit. Other remnants of the pioneer settlements, such as a blacksmith shop and an old schoolhouse, are protected in the park.

Aside from the orchards in Fruita and the carefully maintained lawns in the park and campground, most of surrounding Wayne County is sagebrush country. Cottonwoods, willows, and tamarisks fight for water along the river, but the tamarisk, an exotic plant introduced to the area in the 1930s, is more aggressive and pushes out native plants. Pinion pine and Utah juniper grow throughout this country, with ponderosa pine, Douglas fir, and bristlecone pine wedging into narrow shelves along cliff faces and taking hold in higher elevations.

Game such as sage grouse, chukar, pheasants, cottontail rabbits, waterfowl, deer, elk, gray foxes, cougars, coyotes, snakes, and lizards inhabit the area. The water pockets in Capitol Reef come alive during a rain, with fairy shrimp and other small creatures that have been waiting in the sand for as long as a year for the water to sustain their very short lives, which include hatching and reproducing. The rains foster the cycle of life in the desert, bringing humans here on quests for adventure.

The view near Sundance Trailhead

Dark Canyon Wilderness Complex

SUNDANCE TRAIL

Wading a Desert River Oasis

A river is the string of life that makes the desert palpable. You can descend 1,100 vertical feet in a mile over loose, hot, sandy red rock if you know cool clear water is awaiting your plunge at the bottom.

Located in southeastern Utah near the Hite Marina on the north end of Lake Powell, the Dark Canyon Wilderness Complex is a wonderland of canyons, basins, and soaring cliffs. It is a primitive area with a clear-flowing stream born from natural springs within the canyons. These

43

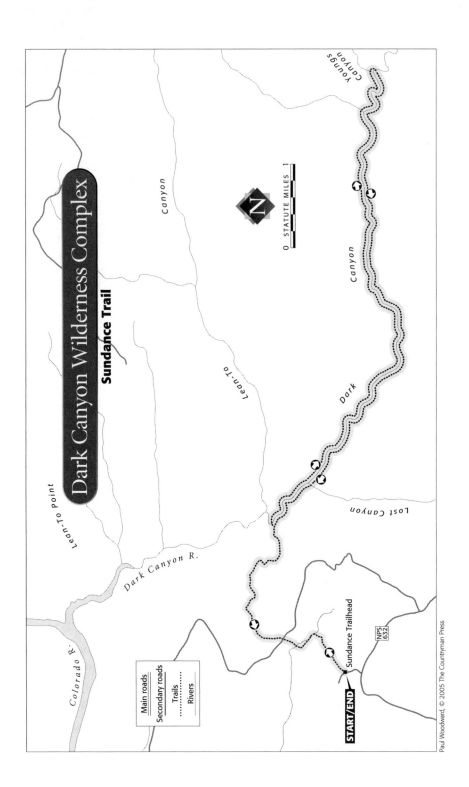

Dark Canyon Wilderness Complex

Sundance Trail

Lean-To point

Colorado R.

Dark Canyon R.

Canyon

Lean-To

Dark

Canyon

Lost Canyon

Youngs Canyon

N

0   STATUTE MILES   1

Main roads
Secondary roads
Trails
Rivers

START/END

Sundance Trailhead

NPS
632

Paul Woodward, © 2005 The Countryman Press

springs supply pools deep enough to swim in and waterfalls high enough to sit under. Canyon walls rise hundreds of feet, exposing 300 million years of geologic history. Where water cuts through, riparian gardens adorn the rock walls.

Dark Canyon offers a remote desert wilderness experience. My travels here have been solitary, quiet, and pristine.

SPORT: Backpacking, camping

RATING: The descent into the canyon and the ascent out are strenuous, but following the stream in the canyon bottom makes for pleasant travel.

DISTANCE: Total distance will be determined by how far you follow the stream up canyon.

TIME: Two or three days

GETTING THERE: From Salt Lake City, head south on I-15 until you reach Exit 259 for Manti/Price. Follow US 6 to Green River, then go west on I-70 just long enough to connect to UT 24 heading south to Hanksville, where you'll turn south on UT 95 to Hite. You can stop for local information, bathrooms, and water at the Hite Ranger Station in the Glen Canyon National Recreation Area next to Lake Powell. The drive takes 4.5 to 5 hours from Salt Lake City and covers 273 miles.

To get to the Sundance Trailhead, turn south from the ranger station, continuing down UT 95. At a quarter mile, take the red dirt road off to the left—NPS 632. It's passable without four-wheel drive, though rain and mud may hamper progress. Stay left along the entire road. It is 4.1 miles to the first junction and 6.4 additional miles to a sign for the Sundance Trailhead. The road is unimproved, and the trailhead parking area is obvious.

TRAIL: The Sundance Trail is the primary access route into the lower portion of Dark Canyon. The trailhead has a trip register and an information board.

A Dark Canyon waterfall

The first 2 miles from the parking area to the rim descend gradually over an easy stretch of cairned trail consisting of rock and sand. Before descending into Dark Canyon you should take a moment to enjoy the bird's-eye view of the canyon from the rim. There is no water available at the trailhead or along the trail until you reach the stream on the canyon floor. Definitely bring water to drink on the climb down.

From the rim, the trail becomes more difficult to decipher; there are cairns going in all directions. If you follow the cairns and trail to the right you will be able to drop into the canyon without climbing gear. But if you miss those, you may find yourself unable to proceed, blocked by cliffs you can't descend without ropes. If you have a GPS, use the following coordinate as a marker from which to start for the cairns to the right: UTM 12 S 0571134 E/4190671 N.

If you don't have a GPS, just stay alert. The trail is steep and primitive and 50 percent loose talus slope. It's a very strenuous descent, made worse by the thought of climbing out again. From the rim you drop 1,120 vertical feet in a mile, then travel another third of a mile along the canyon floor to reach the stream.

The stream makes for a cool refreshing path, but if you don't want to walk it there are trails on one side or the other all the way upstream.

The length of your trip will depend on how much exploring you wish to do. Follow the stream up canyon to access Lean To Canyon (UTM 12 572162 E/4190622 N), Lost Canyon (UTM 12 572520 E/4189798 N), or Youngs Canyon (UTM 12 580249 E/4188939 N). Three-quarters of the water in the main stream comes from springs up Youngs Canyon, so you'll find deeper and deeper pools as you progress along the path. It's almost 8 miles (one way) from your first contact with the stream in Dark Canyon to Youngs Canyon.

MAXIMUM GROUP SIZE: The group limit is 15, and parties of eight or more must make an advance reservation with the BLM.

CAMPING: Camping is permitted in previously established campsites, though there are no officially maintained campsites in the canyon. Do not create new sites or camp at rock art panels or alcoves. Leave No

Trace camping is a must. Bring bags to carry out all toilet paper and garbage. Dump liquid garbage at least 200 feet from water sources. Even though the canyon stream is usually full of water, it always requires filtering.

SEASON: The best times are March through June and September through October.

PERMITS: No permits are required, but large groups need to make reservations with the BLM.

FEES: No fees.

CLOTHING AND EQUIPMENT: You'll be much happier on the steep trip into and out of the canyon if you have a compact, internal-frame backpack. You will also need a water filter and water bottles. Rodents and squirrels can make their way into your campsite, so bring bags and rope to hang your food at night and when you're out of camp.

Campfires are allowed, but backpacking stoves are highly recommended. Bring swimsuits or quick-dry clothing if you plan to jump in the pools and waterfalls along the way. And bring a hat to shield your face from the sun if traveling in the hotter months. Mosquitoes hatch early in the canyon, so be prepared with repellant. Later in June you won't have as many problems with bugs. Sunscreen, a good pair of sunglasses, and a couple of bottles of sport drink (to replace your body's lost electrolytes) are always a good idea, and your feet will be happy in a pair of water sandals.

SUGGESTED ITINERARY

DAY 1: Make your descent into the canyon and begin the hunt for the perfect campsite. Set up your base camp before heading out to explore. There are a few wonderfully shady rock alcoves in which to rest and plenty of nice pools for cooling off or filtering water.

Setting up camp on the canyon floor

DAY 2: You'll likely be up early, as the canyon is wide enough that the sun will hit your tent soon after daybreak. Once the temperature hits 100 degrees in the tent, you can't exit fast enough. Have breakfast, re-hang your food in a tree, and head toward Youngs Canyon to find the deepest pools in the Dark Canyon Complex.

Follow the stream up canyon and enjoy jumping into pools off cliffs or sitting beneath waterfalls. Trek through the stream and climb up rock faces to make your way 8 miles to the mouth of Youngs, a major water source. Day two will be a high-mileage day if you decide to go all the way up to Youngs and then back to camp.

DAY 3: Rest your feet, play cards in the shade, and prepare for the ascent out of the canyon. Dunk yourself in a pool of cool water before the grueling 1,120-foot climb up the final rock-strewn slope. Enjoy the trek out.

RESOURCES

USEFUL WEB SITES AND PHONE NUMBERS
Monticello BLM office: 435-587-1500
Manti–La Sal National Forest, Monticello Ranger District: 435-587-2041

A LITTLE HISTORY, GEOLOGY, FLORA, AND FAUNA

Virtually all life in the desert congregates along rivers. People, plants, and animals are all drawn to the waterways. The rivers appear as green streaks running through the monochromatic browns of sand, rock, and sage.

The Dark Canyon Complex has harbored life in its moist canyon bottoms for centuries. This large canyon system begins on a plateau 8,800 feet above sea level and descends to 3,700 feet, cutting through layers of sandstone and limestone. In the northeast section, Butler Wash, Ruin Park, and Beef Basin contain granaries and remnants of stone buildings from the Paleo-Native Americans that made their home in the area hundreds of years ago. If you find ancient sites, please treat them with respect and don't remove anything. The wood, adobe, and stone in the ruins are over seven hundred years old, and though they appear well preserved, they're extremely fragile.

In the 1870s, cowboys from Texas and New Mexico came here for the lush grass and plentiful water in the canyon bottoms. They brought herds of longhorn cattle to fatten on the area, but they did not stay. The first real settlers were the families that founded Bluff, Monticello, and Blanding in the 1880s and '90s. One of these settlers, J. A. Scorup, built one of the largest ranching companies in the state. Dark Canyon was at the heart of his operation.

In 1946 the area came under BLM management, but it wasn't designated a primitive area until 1970. A few years later the National Park Service placed the adjoining land on its suggested wilderness list. In 1982 the Dark Canyon Complex was designated a Wilderness Study Area, and in 1984 President Reagan signed Utah's National Forest Wilderness Act, which affected the upper section of the Complex. Currently, the BLM manages the lower end of the canyon—including the hike described here—as the Dark Canyon Primitive Area.

The natural springs and streams flowing through the tributary basins are a defining aspect of the area. Lower Dark Canyon has a clear stream with emerald pools and waterfalls flowing through and beneath the rocks and cottonwoods, the sandstone, and the soaring cliffs.

At higher levels, pinion, juniper, and ponderosa pine combine with desert shrub to make habitat for mountain lions, black bears, mule deer, bighorn sheep, porcupines, ringtail cats, bobcats, coyotes, and a variety of birds. Mexican spotted owls and peregrine falcons—both endangered species—inhabit the area. Rodents such as wood rats make their nests in rock piles and crevices, while reptiles like short-horned lizards stalk through sand and over stone.

Dark Canyon provides the opportunity to explore for weeks among canyons that connect with many more canyons. Groups with more time often start from the eastern end of the Complex and take a week to hike from Woodenshoe Canyon through to the Sundance Trailhead. If you have some of that Lewis & Clark spirit, you'll find Dark Canyon an untrammeled and extensive place to explore.

The Maze District of Canyonlands National Park

San Rafael Swell

 CHUTE OF MUDDY CREEK

A Walk Down a Million-Year-Old Path

The best and most daunting aspects of the San Rafael Swell are one and the same—remoteness. One of the few wild and unregulated places left in the country, the Swell is an oasis for anyone who resents the need for permits or wants to pick up and head into the wilderness at the last minute. The area includes 2,000 square miles of public land, most of it unmarred by trails.

Dominated by the jagged uplift of the San Rafael Reef, the Swell is an unmarked wilderness of canyons, buttes, pinnacles, and mesas eroded

53

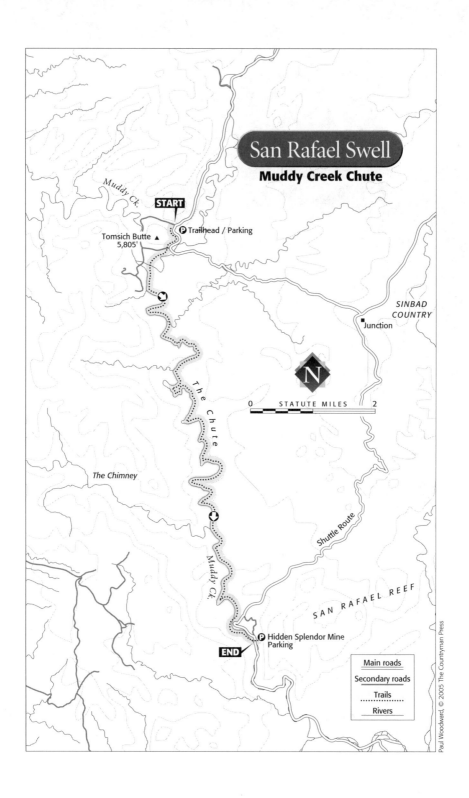

San Rafael Swell
Muddy Creek Chute

Muddy Ck.

START

Trailhead / Parking

Tomsich Butte ▲
5,805'

*SINBAD
COUNTRY*

■ Junction

N

0   STATUTE MILES   2

The Chute

The Chimney

Shuttle Route

Muddy Ck.

SAN RAFAEL REEF

Hidden Splendor Mine
Parking

END

| Main roads |
| Secondary roads |
| Trails |
| Rivers |

Paul Woodward, © 2005 The Countryman Press

into an uplift. This high desert land has views that inspire and trails that you can follow for weeks without seeing another soul. Because of the lack of infrastructure, you must be completely self-sufficient here. Rescue is far away. Vertical-walled canyons reach depths of 1,500 feet. Be prepared both with gear and knowledge when you step into this varied land of old uranium mines, sandstone formations, dirt roads, and panoramic vistas that rival any national park.

The Chute of Muddy Creek is located in the southern section of the San Rafael Swell, entrenched between steep Coconino sandstone cliffs. Your trek down the Muddy includes a few miles at the beginning and end that aren't within the towering walls of the chute. These open desert stretches allow for hiking along the banks as well as in the creek.

The Muddy is one of three rivers that carved the canyons of the Swell over the past millennia. It's most often mid-calf deep, with a few holes that might come up to your waist and long stretches that just lick your ankles. I have chosen the Chute of the Muddy as the introduction to the San Rafael Swell due to the sheer magnitude of the chute walls. Equally important is the refreshing aspect of exploring an arid desert landscape along a green, cool path.

SPORT: Backpacking, river hiking

RATING: The depth of the water will determine the difficulty and speed of travel, but the creek obviously flows downhill so there is no tough elevation gain. This is comfortable river walking.

DISTANCE: It's 3.5 miles from the trailhead to the campsite at the mouth of the Chute of the Muddy. The Chute is approximately 9.5 miles long. It's an additional 3 miles from the exit of the Chute to Hidden Splendor Mine, where you'll have left your shuttle car for this one-way trek (two vehicles required).

TIME: Two days

GETTING THERE: From Salt Lake City, head south on I-15 for 116 miles to Exit 188 at Scipio. Take US 50 for 27 miles to the junction with I-70 at Salina. Head east on I-70 toward Green River for approximately 88 miles. It's possible to see the Swell on the right at various times.

Take Exit 129 and turn right onto the dirt frontage road, UT 24 and Goblin Valley/Temple Mountain Road, which you'll follow around to the west. After 10.2 miles, take the right fork in the road signed RED CANYON/TAN SEEP. The road comes to a T-junction 3.8 miles farther along. Go right, following the sign for Red Canyon/McKay Flat. A mile later veer left and continue for 8.6 miles to the Hidden Splendor Mine junction.

The left fork leads to Hidden Splendor Mine, where you'll leave your shuttle car at a flat parking area atop the butte. It is signed with a trailhead kiosk. The Hidden Splendor airstrip is here as well, marked with a red windsock on a tall pole (UTM S 12 0503537/4268696; elevation 4,828). It's hard to miss.

Hiking through the Chute

After parking your shuttle vehicle, drive back to the junction and take a right toward Tomsich Butte. Views of the Swell are staggering in this section. The road runs along a steep edge as you descend. At the next fork, head right toward Hondoo Arch. Tomsich Butte and the trailhead of the same name are 1 mile from this point.

When you arrive at the trailhead kiosk and the shady cottonwood tree you'll see Hondoo Arch to the left. You can park here or head south on a red dirt road for an additional 0.3 mile to another parking area (UTM S 12 0500200/4281130; elevation 5,051). Keep in mind that if you don't drive the road you will be hiking down it anyway.

TRAIL: The trail, where there is one, is nothing more than a light footpath, but you'll mostly be walking directly in the creek. The path

The Muddy from Hidden Splendor Trailhead

varies from hard pack to rock to sand. (See the suggested itinerary below for specific trail directions and waypoints.)

The key word on the Swell is navigation. You definitely need a GPS or a compass. Hiking the Chute of the Muddy is one of the easier routes to take here, because with the exception of a few hundred yards getting to and from your shuttle vehicles, you will follow Muddy Creek the entire way.

OPTIONAL ACTIVITIES: There are a number of canyoneering opportunities within the San Rafael Swell. Technical canyoneering is practiced using a no-bolt ethic. Be wary if you find bolts already in place; the rock is weak and crumbles unexpectedly. Most canyoneering in the Swell will be hot and dry.

Please remember that the narrow canyons within the Swell are very dangerous and prone to flash floods. At times, the water can rise as much as 50 feet up the canyon walls, and when you're in a slot canyon there is no place to go. Be diligent, know the weather forecast, and watch the sky.

Flash floods are particularly hazardous because they can even occur during sunny weather if it's raining somewhere else in the drainage.

MAXIMUM GROUP SIZE: The BLM designates no maximum group size, but you should follow the backcountry ethics of limiting parties to no larger than 12.

CAMPING: Most camping in the Swell is primitive. There are few established sites, so clean all campsites to leave no trace of their existence. Build fires with downed wood only and scatter ashes.

Hidden Splendor Mine Campground is located at the end of the Chute and consists of nothing more than a few fire rings. There are some nice views of the Muddy from the top, but camping closer to the river offers more seclusion.

SEASON: March through April and September through October are the best months. May and early June are off limits, except for expert kayakers, as water levels from runoff may quadruple in those months. The normal average water flow in the Muddy between October and March stays around 20–30 cubic feet per second (cfs), quickly peaks at 90–100 cfs for a few weeks in May and June, and then drops to 10–15 cfs during the summer.

When we did the Chute in March the water was running at 10 cfs, and it was most often ankle or calf deep with an occasional dip to the knee.

PERMITS AND FEES: None.

CLOTHING AND EQUIPMENT: A reliable water-filtering system is a must. The Muddy is just that, muddy. It's too silty to actually filter unless you use a ceramic filter system and let the sand settle out first. Your only other option for drinking water is adding iodine. I've used both techniques. If you're only going in for a couple of days, pack in good water and sport drinks, so filtering will be less of a hassle. When using iodine, add six drops per quart and let the water sit for 30 minutes.

As mentioned earlier, you'll need navigational tools. And don't forget sunscreen, sunglasses, and first-aid supplies. You must be able to take care of any possible problems on your own, as help will be a long way off. Common sense is your best guide in such a remote area; make the extra effort to stay safe.

A bandana can be used as a head wrap, a bandage, and even a tourniquet, but you can also use it as a first-round filter for river water. Place the bandana over the top of the bottle and pour water through it. The worst of the silt will be kept out.

Bring water sandals for your time in the river. Depending on the season in which you visit, you may want to bring warm clothing. In canyon shade the water can be intensely cold. A good outer layer of insulation will help trap body heat and reduce your chances of hypothermia. On our March trip, we wore warm winter beanies, fleece jackets, and socks with our sandals. During warmer months we just wear shorts and T-shirts. The water temperature is much warmer in the summer than in the spring.

A walking stick can be helpful during stream crossings and as a depth probe when hiking down the river. Deer flies can be a real beast, so load up on strong bug repellant.

SUGGESTED ITINERARY

DAY 1: Drop off your shuttle car at Hidden Splendor Mine, and then drive to Tomsich Butte Trailhead (UTM 12 S 0500124/4281730; elevation 5,025). Make your way to Muddy Creek, which you can hear as you hike south. Follow the Muddy another 3.6 miles (UTM 12 S 0501644/4278390) to the last piece of flat ground before the Chute. This is a great place to set up camp.

You'll be at the base of a plateau that has a foot trail leading up it. After establishing camp, day-hike onto the plateau to see some beautiful views out over the Swell, as well as down into the Chute off the south side of the plateau.

DAY 2: Today is your foray into the Chute. At times it opens up to wider ground, but most of the 9 miles will put you between high canyon walls. You can't afford to be in the Chute during a flash flood. If it looks like rain, stay out. If the weather is good, head on in. The trail is the creek. Simply follow it through the fabulous narrow walls and the occasional open expanse. Your destination is Hidden Splendor Mine on the other side of the Chute.

RESOURCES

TOURS AND GUIDES
Guides for the San Rafael Swell are hard to come by. Hondoo Rivers and Trails takes clients on horseback rides through the Swell, and they will charter special hiking trips as requested. Contact them at 1-800-332-2696, hondoo@color-country.net, or www.hondoo.com.

USEFUL WEB SITES AND PHONE NUMBERS
BLM Price Field Office: 435-636-3600
Canyoneering USA: www.canyoneeringusa.com/utah
USGS Stream Flow for Muddy Creek: http://waterdata.usgs.gov/ut/nwis/uv/?site_no=09330500&PARAmeter_cd=00065,00060,00010,72020

A LITTLE HISTORY, GEOLOGY, FLORA, AND FAUNA

By A.D. 1300, the Indian tribe currently recognized as the Fremont had left the canyons of the San Rafael Swell. The best remaining evidence of their existence here is the remnant rock art panels and a cliff dwelling with masonry walls found high on a cliff. The Ute and Paiute Indians were the next to move into the area, but there is little evidence of their habitation.

In the 1800s, the Spaniards and Mexicans established the Old Spanish Trail through the Swell for the purpose of trading cattle and horses. The region was used as a grazing area by early pioneers who populated the West. In 1847 Mormon pioneers, the ones responsible for developing all the small surrounding towns, moved into the Swell, bringing herds of cattle with them.

The San Rafael Swell has been repeatedly overlooked for wilderness protection because of its value for mineral development and grazing. It is currently multiple-use land, which includes motorized vehicles and grazing. The Swell has a history rich in uranium mining, and many old mines still exist in the area. For safety reasons, it isn't wise to enter any of these mines. The network of dirt roads built by prospectors and miners in the 1950s still provide the best access into the Swell.

The geology of the Swell can be summed up in two words: upheaval and erosion. Eighty miles long and 30 wide, the San Rafael Swell is part of the Colorado Plateau, in a portion called the Canyon Lands section. Hundreds of millions of years ago a number of uplifts, including the Uncompahgre Uplift, formed a bulge in the earth's crust, creating the Swell. The sawtooth-edged San Rafael Reef forms a partial 50-mile Navajo and Wingate sandstone ring around the eastern edge of the plateau. An uplift forced this section of earth into an almost vertical fold. The depression inside the reef is called the Sinbad area.

Eons of sea-level variation, glacial forming and melting, temperature variations, and other geologic processes created the stratifications of colored rock within the Swell. All the viewable geologic features here were formed in the Jurassic and Triassic periods, 150 million to 200 million years ago. The lighter layers were deposited underwater, when the lack of tidal movements allowed salts to settle. The darker layers were most often deposited above water.

Deep canyons formed as the Colorado Plateau continued to rise and the rivers cut slowly through the newly created dome, or swell. There are three rivers within the Swell: the San Rafael, the Price, and the Muddy. The Chute of the Muddy is one of the canyons formed during the same millennia that the Swell was formed. The Muddy River joins the Fremont River to the southeast to form the Dirty Devil River.

Cryptobiotic soil is prevalent in many parts of the Swell. Watch for these areas and make sure to choose other walking paths. Cryptobiotic soil has a dark, raised appearance. If you're not watching carefully, you can miss it entirely. (See the Introduction for further information on the cryptobiotic soil ecosystem.)

The descent into Mystery Canyon

Zion National Park

 MYSTERY AND KEYHOLE CANYONS

Dropping into Beauty and Intrigue

Zion, which means "peaceful resting place," is anything but peaceful when one embarks on slot canyon expeditions that require trekking through frigid pools of water, rappelling off 100-foot cliffs, and sliding through tight slots. But peace is not what canyoneers look for; they want adventure. Utah canyoneering is about the challenge of finding one's way through the narrow slot canyons carved by the waterways of the West and the obstacles that stand in the way—boulder jams,

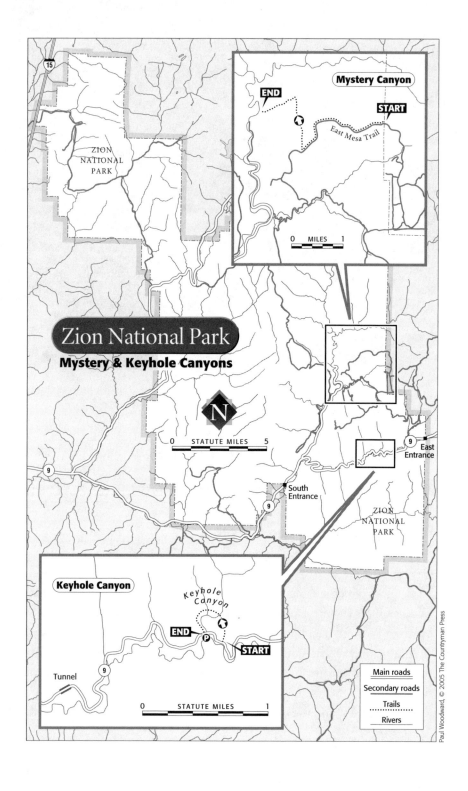

Mystery Canyon

END

START

East Mesa Trail

0 MILES 1

Zion National Park

Mystery & Keyhole Canyons

ZION NATIONAL PARK

N

0 STATUTE MILES 5

9

9 East Entrance

South Entrance

9

ZION NATIONAL PARK

Keyhole Canyon

Keyhole Canyon

END P START

Tunnel

9

0 STATUTE MILES 1

Main roads
Secondary roads
Trails
Rivers

logjams, cliff walls, waterfalls, and pools of water both stagnant and clear.

Mystery and Keyhole Canyons are not only two of the most beautiful and interesting slot canyons in Zion National Park, they are also world class. Zion has been valued for its spiritual resources since humans first laid eyes on the magnificence of the area and its red sandstone cliffs. There is a feeling of grandeur here that is difficult to comprehend until you round the curve on UT 9 and catch your first glimpse of the Park.

Mystery Canyon was chosen for this adventure because of its beauty, the quality of the canyon and obstacles, and the reasonable level of technical skill required. Keyhole Canyon is a short but intense technical adventure. After your half-day of canyoneering is finished, you'll still have time for a bike ride, one of Zion's famous hikes, or lounging at camp with your legs propped up. Both canyons offer five-star fun.

SPORT: Canyoneering

RATING: Mystery Canyon (rated −3BIII in the Canyon Rating System) is a technical canyoneering adventure that combines a steep hiking descent, boulder problems, a couple of ice-cold swims, and up to 12 rappels. Two of these are 100-plus feet, the final one dropping over a waterfall into the beautiful Narrows of the Virgin River. It requires two 50-meter ropes and appropriate rappel gear. This canyon should only be attempted by experienced rappellers. It is bolted in all the appropriate places.

Keyhole Canyon (rated 3BI in the Canyon Rating System) is an intimate slot canyon that also requires appropriate rappel gear and experience. Aptly named, it's as thin as a key slot with plenty of curves and drops. There are three rappels, a number of swimming holes (including a chest-high stretch that varies with runoff and is very cold at any time of year), tree trunks, and boulder problems. This canyon is appropriate for beginners, but still requires previous knowledge of rappelling technique and rope setup.

The final rappel into the Narrows from Mystery Canyon

TIME: Eight or nine hours for Mystery Canyon; two hours for Keyhole Canyon

GETTING THERE: To reach Zion National Park from Salt Lake City, head south on I-15 toward Las Vegas for 280 miles. Take Exit 27 and go toward Toquerville/Hurricane on UT 17 for 6 miles. Turn left onto UT 9 and follow it for 6.2 miles. Turn left again onto Kolob Road/100 E. for 0.4 mile until it becomes Kolob Road, then continue for an additional 7.3 miles. Turn right to stay on Kolob Road and follow it for another mile to Springdale and Zion National Park. The drive takes around five hours and covers 303.25 miles.

Mystery Canyon. You can attempt Mystery Canyon from a number of trailheads. The East Mesa Trailhead is the easiest option physically, but it requires a car shuttle. A logistically easier but longer route starts at Weeping Rock Trailhead, which is accessible via the shuttle up the Zion Canyon Scenic Drive. It includes an additional 2,400 feet of elevation gain, but returns as a loop hike.

East Mesa Trailhead is accessed from the south entrance of Zion by following UT 9 (Zion Mount Carmel Highway) 4.5 miles to the tunnel, 1.1 miles through the tunnel, and then 5.4 miles on to the east entrance. Continue east for 2.4 miles on UT 9 until you reach the North Fork junction. A small sign marks the road. Turn left and drive 5.2 miles to the sign for Zion Ponderosa Resort. Turn left and enter the Zion Ponderosa.

The dirt roads from here are two-wheel-drive accessible, but might by difficult when wet. A number of spur roads intersect with the main road, so be careful not to get off on one of these. Continue straight on the main road toward Observation Point. About a mile in, a spur road joins from the right; stay left. Shortly after, go right at the T-junction. Bear right another 0.1 mile farther on at the fork.

Continue on the main road, ignoring the next spur road that enters on the right. Stay left at the next fork, and then bear right at the one immediately following. Ignore the spur roads again for the next 0.1 mile. Bear left at the next fork, and then cross Fir Road and continue straight. At the next fork, head right toward Observation Point. In 0.8 mile go left at the fork and look for the trailhead. Park at the fence, which marks the border with Zion National Park. Walk south a short way along the fence to the entrance point and trail.

Keyhole Canyon. Keyhole Canyon is much easier to reach. Simply park at a roadside pullout 1.9 miles from the end of the short tunnel along the Zion Mount Carmel Highway (UT 9). The trail is directly across the road.

ǁ TRAIL: MYSTERY CANYON. To enter Mystery Canyon via the one-way route starting at East Mesa Trailhead, park your car at the trailhead (UTM 12 S 0331488/4129463; elevation 6,516) and head south along the fence until you come to the trail opening, which should be obvious. The trail extends 1.8 miles before dropping down into the canyon. The trail into Mystery takes off to the right and is completely unmarked (UTM 12 S 0328903/4128652; elevation 6,794). Use the big white wall, which is visible across the canyon, as a trail indicator to show you when to head down into Mystery. Be careful not to head down the wrong canyon here, as each year there are a couple of groups that drop in at the wrong spot and then require rescue.

There is another trail with rocks placed in front of it just past the correct trail; don't take it. The correct trail is a red packed footpath that descends into Mystery Canyon. It becomes a steep, thin, exposed, and rocky trail heading to the right.

Descend into the canyon using tree roots and any other handholds you can find. You'll need traction, so wear good hiking boots. As you make your way down you'll come across rock jams. There are usually vague trails to the right that will help you get up and around these obstacles.

After the descent the canyon flattens out and runs along tall cliff walls. The shade and the mosses growing from the rocks give it a serene feel. Follow the bottom of the canyon through to the last rappel.

The route is well bolted. There are four rappels down the main slot: R1: 45 feet; R2: 30 feet; R3: 12 feet; R4: 50 feet. The walls then open up a bit, and there are a couple of short rappels and boulder obstacles before you come to a wash. The wash opens up into a sandy hiking trail that runs into a big mountain of rocks formed by a massive rockslide. Make your way over the mountain of sand and rocks and descend down the other side.

Next, you do a couple more short rappels, then stop and secure all your gear in dry bags before arriving at the 110-foot rappel into Mystery Springs. It starts from an exposed ledge, but there is a hand line to follow out to the anchors while you set up your belay. You drop right into the spring at the end of the belay. Just swim backward to bring the rope with you to the edge. The water is clear.

There are a few more obstacles to descend before the final spectacular 120-foot rappel down a thin waterfall into the Narrows. Walk down the Narrows for a quarter mile to the riverside trail, which will take you to your shuttle car or to a shuttle to town.

Navigating Keyhole Canyon

Keyhole Canyon. To reach Keyhole Canyon, park at the pullout past the small tunnel and walk 100 yards up the road toward the east entrance. You'll see a spot on the left where you can drop down into a sandy wash. Head up the wash toward the sandstone beehive to the left (UTM 12 S 0331383/4121701; elevation 5,569). A sandy trail descends on the left side of the hive; follow it to the bottom.

Keyhole Canyon is the small slot directly to your left as you hit the bottom (UTM 12 S 0331375/4121745; elevation 5,601). The first portion of the canyon is dry. After a few rappels it will abruptly end and open up. It begins again in another 20 yards, and you'll use the webbing and rappel rings strung to a ponderosa pine directly in front of the slot to lower yourself into the next phase of the canyon. Do not attempt to rappel from, or to down climb, the tree lodged in the canyon.

Next there are a series of rappels, some as long as 65 feet, a bit of down climbing, pools of stagnant water, and a 3-foot-wide corridor filled with cold water. This is the flooded hallway, and it requires a long swim through a narrow slot where the water can be chest high. Push against the walls with your hands and feet to propel yourself forward.

The slot ends shortly after this last swim, kicking you out into the sunshine right next to the road. It's a very short walk to your car.

Note: All narrow canyons are potential flash flood zones. Cold water and strong currents can be life threatening, so make adequate preparations and use good judgment. Flash floods often come from storms miles away. Check the current weather forecast at the permit office before heading out. You are responsible for your own safety.

OPTIONAL ACTIVITIES: Road biking along the scenic drives in Zion is popular. Mountain biking in the Park is off limits, but it's one of the primary outdoor activities in surrounding areas. Gooseberry Mesa and the Rim Routes are the most popular areas. Gooseberry Mesa is a tabletop mesa just west of Zion. The trail system combines slickrock and single track into a biking playground of sorts. Intermediate to advanced riders will enjoy it the most.

The Rim Routes are located one mile west of Virgin. There are a handful of trails in this area that link up with one another, making it possible to choose rides of various length. These are desert trails that require a minimum of technical skill, yet they can be ridden hard and fast by advanced bikers. The JEM Trail and Hurricane Rim Trail are popular rides in this area.

The JEM Trail is a cross-desert, double-track dirt road of 12.7 miles that narrows to single track on the descent. The Hurricane Rim Trail follows the Virgin River, at times offering an amazing view of the river hundreds of feet below. You ride this rim with only a few feet, sometimes less, between your bike tire and the edge. This trail is a little over 8 miles one way and takes just a few hours to complete.

The bike shops in Springdale have maps of the area.

MAXIMUM GROUP SIZE: Permits can be obtained for up to 12 people, but group sizes for canyoneering should be kept small in order to avoid congestion. These are popular canyons with multiple groups going through each day, and rappelling clogs can develop quickly. Suggested group size is no more than four.

CAMPING: There are two campgrounds in Zion National Park: South and Watchman. Both are next to the visitors' center and the south entrance of the Park on the main road. They are first come, first served.

South Campground is open all year and has 180 campsites, a dump station, bathrooms, picnic tables, fire pits, and running water. Potable water is available from a pump. Watchman Campground is open from March 15 to November 1 and has 170 sites with the same amenities as South. Fees are $16 per night and spaces usually fill up by 11 AM during the busy season. Campers must bring their own firewood, as collecting wood in the Park is prohibited. There are no RV hook-ups.

Backcountry camping is allowed on a limited basis and a permit is required. Permits cost $5 per night, with group size limited to 12. No campfires are allowed. Permits are issued at the visitors' center.

SEASON: The prime season is May through October. Water levels in the Narrows must be below 140 cfs before permits are issued for Mystery

Canyon. July and August bring summer thunderstorms, and flash flood danger may cancel your trip during these months.

Ⓟ **PERMITS:** Backcountry permits are necessary for all canyons requiring the use of descending gear or ropes. The person who obtains the permit must be 18 or older and must actually be on the trip. Permits for Mystery Canyon are in high demand and can be difficult to get if you're not on the ball. They're also dependent on the flow in the Narrows. When the water level is low enough, 12 permits a day are issued.

Permits for Mystery Canyon can be obtained in four different ways:

1. Zion Express Permits can be obtained online (www.nps.gov/zion) for "frequent fliers."

2. Lottery applications can be drawn for position. (See the calendar schedule below.) The lottery runs for trip dates between April and October.

3. Walk-in permits can be obtained the day before or the day of your trip, but there is no availability guarantee.

4. After the lottery has taken place an online calendar shows which days still have permits available. You can make reservations for a permit through this calendar web page.

Permits for Keyhole Canyon can be obtained through an online calendar reservation (www.nps.gov/zion) or at walk-in. Fifty permits a day are available. Visitors with reservations still need to pick up a backcountry permit, available in person the day before or the day of your trip.

Ⓢ **FEES:** The Park entry fee is $20. Specific permit fees range from $10 to $20 depending on how many are in your group. The nonrefundable lottery fee is $5. The nonrefundable calendar reservation fee is $5.

🆃 **CLOTHING AND EQUIPMENT:** You'll need two 50-meter ropes for Mystery Canyon and 130 feet of rope for Keyhole. You'll also need harnesses, rappel devices, locking carabiners, and webbing. A rope bag makes it easy to collect the rope after each of the many short rappels.

For a trip in:	Lottery applications must be received during the month of:	Calendar reservations become available:
January	–	November 5
February	–	December 5
March	–	January 5
April	January	February 5
May	February	March 5
June	March	April 5
July	April	May 5
August	May	June 5
September	June	July 5
October	July	August 5
November	–	September 5
December	–	October 5

Shoes with good traction are necessary for the descent into Mystery Canyon, and you'll need water shoes or sandals for the lower water-filled portions. Bring a dry bag for things you don't want to get wet, and include mosquito repellant for both canyons. Sunscreen, lunch, and plenty to drink will keep you happy. Bring a jacket to prevent any risk of hypothermia as you exit the cold pools.

SUGGESTED ITINERARY

DAY 1: It takes a full day to negotiate the wonders of Mystery Canyon.

DAY 2: Keyhole Canyon fills a half-day slot, which leaves time for hiking or biking in the Zion area. Catching a movie at the big

IMAX screen in the Park is a nice way to relax after a day in the canyon.

RESOURCES

GUIDES AND OUTFITTERS
Zion Rock & Mountain Guides: 435-772-3305; www.zionrockguides.com; rents canyoneering and camping gear, teaches classes on canyoneering and rappelling, and provide shuttle services
Red Rock Shuttles: 435-635-9104
Zion Canyon Transportation: 1-877-772-3303
Zion Cycles, LLC: 435-772-0400; www.zioncycles.com; rents bikes
Springdale Cycle Tours: 1-800-776-2099; www.springdalecycles.com; provides bike rentals and guided backcountry cycle tours

USEFUL WEB SITES AND PHONE NUMBERS
Zion National Park web site: www.nps.gov/zion
Park Headquarters: 435-772-3256 or 435-772-0170 (backcountry information line); ZION_park_information@nps.gov

A LITTLE HISTORY, GEOLOGY, FLORA, AND FAUNA

Zion received its name from the first white settlers in the area, the Mormons. Early visitors, like the Methodist minister Frederick Vining Fisher, added names such as Great White Throne and Angels Landing to the landscape. Paiutes, the Indian tribe native to the area, have their own legends about the spirits that inhabit this land of 2,000- to 3,000-foot cliffs. Additional names like the Altar of Sacrifice; the Three Patriarchs: Abraham, Isaac, and Jacob; and West Temple also attest to the awe and reverence this sandstone canyon evokes.

Zion Canyon is the best-known feature in the Park's 147,000 acres of sculpted sandstone canyons and high desert plateaus. The Virgin River follows, or carves, the canyon floor. This area is currently accessed via a shuttle system, implemented by the National Park Service to keep congestion and air pollution to a minimum given its nearly three million visitors a year. The paved Riverside Walk runs next to the Virgin River before ending at the Narrows, the deep canyon the river has cut into the plateau.

The Narrows is the most popular and frequented area of the Park and serves as the exit point for Mystery Canyon. From its source 8,700 feet above sea level just north of Zion, the Virgin River descends 7,500 feet, carving the canyons as it goes. It scours the canyon floor, carrying away a million tons of sediment each year. This sediment eventually goes into Lake Mead on the Colorado River.

Aside from the Virgin River, only a few Zion streams have water all year. Most water sources are from seasonal flooding. These flows fill side canyons in Zion from time to time, and the small pools you pass through when canyoneering come from this runoff or from natural springs.

Cool, shady canyon bottoms provide the right loamy balance for many plants, and hanging gardens are often present on shady walls where porous and dense rock meet up. The American dipper, a year-round resident of Zion, builds its nest in these hanging gardens and behind waterfalls. These little birds can often be seen standing in the water dipping their bodies up and down.

Mule deer are one of the most frequently seen animals in the Park, with the nocturnal ringtail cat, kangaroo rats, short-horned lizards, porcupines, elk, desert bighorn sheep, collared lizards, and tarantulas all present. Mountain lions, though nocturnal and secretive, are prevalent here as well. They play their part in keeping the mule deer population in balance.

Though an attack by a mountain lion has never been reported in Zion, these animals are notorious for picking off small stray animals. Never let children hike alone or lag behind. If you do see a mountain lion, don't run; put your arms up to make yourself appear as large as possible. The cats don't have great eyesight and usually avoid attacking larger prey. Report any sightings, but don't be afraid to venture out just because they call Zion home.

The area we now know as Zion National Park was first established in 1909 as Mukuntuweap National Monument by order of President Taft, after the region was mapped by Deputy Surveyor Leo Snow. *Mukuntuweap* is a Paiute word that was used by John Wesley Powell during his explorations. In 1919 the area was expanded and became Zion National Park. It is made up of 229 square miles, with an elevation ranging from 3,666 to 8,726 feet.

Because of this variation in elevation, Zion is a land with a variety of habitats and life zones. Cool moist plateaus are found at the highest elevations, arid conditions prevail among the slopes and canyon bottoms, and rivers feed lush riparian environs. Each of these zones supports distinct wildlife communities, giving the area an abundance of different flora and fauna. The plateaus above Zion were once filled with old-growth ponderosa pine that has since been harvested.

Zion's human history is marked by artifacts dating to around 7000 B.C., when the Basketmaker culture was present in the area. Later remnants were left by the Ancestral Puebloans who lived in and around Zion until A.D. 1200, when they abandoned the area for unknown reasons. The Southern Paiutes farmed Zion in more recent centuries. There is a belief among these Native Americans that all things are created on an equal level with humans. Each rock, tree, human, and animal has something to share and depends on the others for life. It is said that all things upon this land understand the Paiute language.

The Dominques/Escalante party included the first Europeans to visit the area, although they moved through quickly. When the Mormons settled here, the infusion was rapid and enduring. Mormon pioneers settled Springdale, beginning with Nephi Johnson, a Mormon missionary and scout.

Other Mormon pioneers settled the surrounding communities. They dug irrigation ditches, grazed livestock in the canyons, cultivated crops, and harvested timber for their homes. This was their promised land—a place of refuge. Some fencing, irrigation ditches, and orchards from the 19th-century settlements are still visible. Isaac Behunin, another Mormon pioneer, built the first cabin in the canyon.

The view from Overlook Day Hike

Maze District, Canyonlands National Park

Enter the Challenge of the Labyrinth

Mazes have long been things of wonder, challenge, trial, and torture. They are games, but serious ones. You think you're pretty good with that fancy GPS? Well, few canyon systems in Utah will get you lost and wear you out faster than the Maze District of Canyonlands National Park.

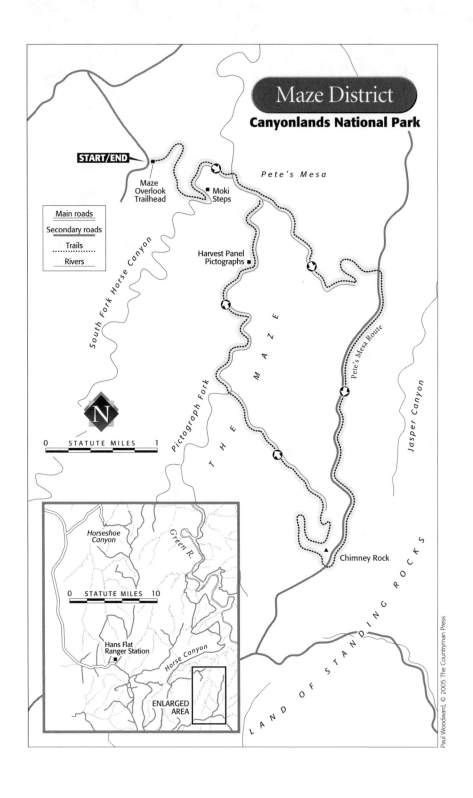

Maze District
Canyonlands National Park

START/END

Maze
Overlook
Trailhead

Moki
Steps

Pete's Mesa

Main roads
Secondary roads
Trails
Rivers

Harvest Panel
Pictographs

South Fork Horse Canyon

Pete's Mesa Route

Jasper Canyon

N

0 STATUTE MILES 1

Pictograph Fork

T H E   M A Z E

Chimney Rock

Horseshoe
Canyon

Green R.

0 STATUTE MILES 10

L A N D   O F   S T A N D I N G   R O C K S

Hans Flat
Ranger Station

Horse Canyon

ENLARGED
AREA

Paul Woodward, © 2005 The Countryman Press

The Maze is a group of five major canyons on the west side of the Green River that branch into hundreds of smaller canyons over roughly 100 square miles. This area provides an extremely isolated, mentally challenging, and physically demanding desert backpacking experience.

For a warm-up to the Maze, we'll start with a half-day hike down into Horseshoe Canyon to see the extensive and rare Barrier Canyon Style pictograph panels. Combined with mountain-bikeable jeep roads down the Flint Trail and across Elaterite Basin on your way to the Maze—and of course backpacking in the Maze itself—this makes for a weekend adventure filled with beauty and intrigue.

When you finally make your way to the trailhead, also referred to as Maze Overlook, you'll quickly realize this is not exactly your typical National Park Service destination. There are no gift shop, no parking lots, no throngs of tourists, and not a single diorama filled with stuffed critters. You'll walk to the edge alone, peer down 600 feet into the Maze, and see endless canyons and side canyons and side canyons of side canyons—all cut into red, white, and orange Cedar Mesa sandstone.

Maze Overlook is just the beginning of an unforgettable two-day backpacking trip through the heart of the Maze. You'll traverse deep canyons, climb to ridgetops for an awesome 360-degree view of Canyonlands that few people ever see, and come out in Pictograph Fork, which contains one of the most unusual pictograph panels in the region.

Add 4×4 roads, jeep roads, and creekbeds you have to drive just to get to the Maze, and you've got one gonzo trip in front of you.

SPORT: Backpacking, hiking, mountain biking, 4×4

RATING: Horseshoe Canyon is easy enough for beginning hikers. Mountain biking down the Flint Trail and across Elaterite Basin to the Maze Overlook is strenuous and requires some advanced biking skills and a solid fitness level. Backpacking in the Maze is strenuous, regardless of the route. And the 4×4 trails are tough, definitely not for first-timers.

DISTANCE: Horseshoe Canyon, 6.5 miles; Maze, 12.9 miles (including the Overlook Loop day hike); mountain bike/4×4 trail from Hans Ranger Station to Maze Overlook, 34 miles

TIME: Horseshoe Canyon, four hours; Maze, two days; mountain bike/4×4 trail from Hans Ranger Station to Maze Overlook, 3–4 hours.

GETTING THERE: The road journey for this trip is a big part of its appeal. It is as remote a road as you're going to get in the lower 48 states. If you're driving a gas-guzzler with a range of less than 260 miles you'll definitely need an extra gas can for this one.

From Salt Lake City, head south on I-15 toward Las Vegas. Merge onto US 6 East via Exit 261 near Spanish Fork, about 50 miles outside Salt Lake City. Stay on US 6 for approximately 129 miles, until you come to the junction with I-70. Go west on I-70 for 8.5 miles to Exit 147 for Hanksville. Continue south for 25 miles.

Between mileposts 136 and 137 you'll see a dirt road to the east. Follow it for 24 miles to a fork. To reach the Horseshoe Canyon Trailhead for the day hike, take the left fork for 5 miles to a signed junction. Then turn right and continue 2 miles to a BLM trailhead and the rim of Horseshoe Canyon.

Pictograph panel

To continue on to the Maze, take the right fork back at the "Y." The road forks again after 7 miles; stay to the left. The dirt road to the Hans Flat Ranger Station is generally well maintained. A toilet, books, and maps are available at Hans Flat, as well as your permit.

Continue 14 additional miles to the top of the Flint Trail. Then descend 3 miles and 1,000 feet down the Flint, backing up as necessary for the switchbacks on this narrow, exposed road. At the bottom you'll head out across the Elaterite Basin for a scenic but rough ride. Follow the signs toward Maze Overlook. It's 15.6 miles from the top of the Flint Trail to the Maze Overlook, but because of the rough roads, plan on two or three hours of driving time. This is a serious 4×4 experience, so don't attempt it without a solid vehicle and some patience.

If you don't have a four-wheel-drive vehicle, talk to the rangers at Hans Flat about accessing Maze Overlook via North Trail Canyon. This adds at least a day to either end of your Maze trip, but it is a viable option.

TRAIL: The key word on this trek is cairns—those small piles of rocks that serve as trail markers. This is a maze, a labyrinth, wall after wall, canyon after canyon, junction after junction, and they all look the same. Some are dead ends, some connect to other canyons, some fork and then fork again. The challenge is finding your way through. All the trails covered in this chapter are well marked with cairns.

Keep your eyes peeled for these "signposts" and you will find your way, but make sure you have a map and compass, and if possible a GPS. With the cairns and the directions and GPS coordinates given below, along with a modicum of orienteering know-how, you should be just fine.

Horseshoe Canyon Trail: The trail to the Great Gallery pictograph panel starts at a BLM trailhead and drops 750 feet in 1 mile. The trail becomes a flat riverbed walk for 2.25 miles to the Great Gallery and three other rock art sites. You then retrace your steps back up to the BLM trailhead. The most difficult part of the trail is the climb out.

Maze Approach: If someone in your party can drive the 4×4 vehicle for the approach to the Maze, the rest can mountain bike the 34-mile double track from Hans Flat down the Flint Trail and out to Maze Overlook. (See "Getting There" above for more details about this road.)

The backpacking adventure from Maze Overlook starts with a 1-mile, Class 4 scramble down a 600-foot cliff into the South Fork of Horse Canyon. While exposed, this scramble has perfect hand and footholds wherever needed. The route is well cairned. You'll have to pass packs down by hand or rope in several sections. (A 30-foot length of thin, light rope is fine.) Once you're in the canyon, locate an appropriate spot for your base camp.

The next adventure within the Maze is the Overlook Loop day hike, a 13.5-mile loop that takes you up onto the rim for an exquisite and extensive view of the Maze, past Jasper Canyon, through Pictograph Fork, and past the Harvest Panel Pictographs.

MAXIMUM GROUP SIZE: Group size is limited to 20 in Horseshoe Canyon. At Maze Overlook, vehicle camping is limited to nine people and three vehicles. For backcountry camping in the Maze, the maximum is five people, with as few vehicles as possible left at the trailhead.

CAMPING: Many hikers camp at the Maze Overlook and simply day-hike into the Maze. This is a beautiful and easier option if you can secure a campsite and permit. Only two campsites are available. The disadvantage is that you can't go very far into the Maze.

Plenty of good campsites are available in the backcountry. The most popular option is to camp at the mouth of Pictograph Fork. This gives you the option of setting up a base camp for a couple of nights and doing day hikes. The only requirement given by the ranger for backcountry camping is that you are out of sight of the Maze Overlook before choosing a campsite. Camping fees are included in your permit fee.

SEASON: Late March through April and late September through October are the best—and most crowded—months, with daytime temperatures in the 60s and 70s. This makes backpacking relatively pleasant, but be aware that spring weather is very unpredictable. A significant amount of the year's precipitation falls in March and April.

In May, daytime temperatures rise into the 80s and 90s. You should have your head examined if you try to do anything physical in here between June and mid-September, when 100-degree days are common.

The view from Overlook Day Hike

Violent afternoon thunderstorms also arrive in July and August. They may force you to cut your trip short, because it's often impossible to drive out on Flint Trail once it's wet. Winter travel is possible if you're coming in from Hite to the south, but daytime temperatures only average in the 30s.

(P) PERMITS: Permits are required for all overnight trips in the Maze District. They can be reserved in advance by calling 435-259-4351 and can be picked up at the Hans Flat Ranger Station.

$ **FEES:** Backcountry permits cost $15 and vehicle camping permits $30.

CLOTHING AND EQUIPMENT: Bring lots of water—at least one gallon per person, per day. On a two-day backpacking trip you should carry two gallons of water on the first day, which is an extra 16 pounds in your pack. This extra weight forces you to be selective with the other items you pack. If you're smart, you'll toss out the three changes of clean underwear, the iPod, and that hardcover book you're reading.

Because water is such an issue, you won't want to waste it cleaning pots. This is a great time to try those eat-in-the-pouch dehydrated meals.

Bring a good hat and sunscreen. As mentioned earlier, a 30-foot length of rope will help with lowering backpacks in at least one place. Because of all the climbing and descending on steep terrain, a smaller, less cumbersome backpack in the 2,500- to 3,000-cubic-inch range will help you feel more secure. If you have the choice of bringing an old pack or a shiny new one, I'd recommend the former. The Maze has been known to wear a hole or two in many a pack. Make sure you bring a tent with bug netting to protect you from the no-see-ums and gnats. And a headlamp can be a lifesaver if you end up climbing out of the Maze in the dark.

SUGGESTED ITINERARY

DAY 1: The adventure begins with a stop at Horseshoe Canyon on the way to the Maze. The Great Gallery, located about 3 miles up Horseshoe Canyon, is one of the great pictograph panels of the Southwest. Three additional pictograph panels are in the canyon: Horseshoe Shelter, High Gallery, and Alcove. You pass them on your way to the Great Gallery.

As you descend into Horseshoe Canyon, look for remnants of an industrious pumping system built by a local sheep rancher in 1939. He used old oil-rig materials to pump water from the canyon floor to the rim. The road makes one big switchback to the west and takes you 500 feet down to the riverbed in roughly a mile. Interesting erosion has taken place in the riverbed rock, which has the appearance of Swiss cheese.

Follow cairns in the riverbed to the southwest. The canyon gradually narrows, and in places the trail cuts a straight line rather than following the exact course of the riverbed. At 1.77 miles, about 40 minutes into the hike, you reach the first panel—High Gallery. Follow a side trail out of the wash on the left side of the canyon to reach the site.

The second site, Horseshoe Shelter, is located 1.96 miles up the trail. Cross the dry riverbed and head only slightly down the wash and to the north to find it. Both petroglyph sites are marked. In 1930, archeologists excavated Horseshoe Shelter and found clay figurines and "trash" that suggested use as far back as A.D. 1, as well as more recent use by Fremont and Ancestral Puebloan (formerly known as Anasazi) cultures. This site once contained several rooms, but only the pictographs remain.

The third panel, the Alcove, is at 2.01 miles. This panel is more difficult to find because you can't see it from the trail (UTM 12 S 0569704/4257261; elevation 4,637). As you come into a rock amphitheater you'll see a large sand ledge. The panel is located atop this ledge. Follow cairns to the site.

At 3.14 miles you come to the Great Gallery, which is easy to locate. Rest on the logs and rocks under a cottonwood tree while you view the panel. A couple of Park Service ammo cans left at the site contain folders with research and history on the Great Gallery, as well as a sign-in book and a set of binoculars for up-close viewing.

All four panels within Horseshoe Canyon represent the style prevalent from 2500 B.C. to A.D. 500. Samples of the rock art within the Great Gallery were dated to 1200 B.C. with AMS radio carbon dating.

Retrace your steps to the trailhead, hop in the car, and make your way back out to the Y-junction that takes you to Hans Flat Ranger Station. Hans Flat lies in an area of cedar trees atop a huge plateau called the Spur, between Millard and Horse Canyons. Stop at the ranger station to get your backcountry permit. The ranger there will explain all the regulations and answer any questions you have.

Whether riding a mountain bike or driving, you continue south from Hans Flat on the sandy and rocky road for 10 miles toward the top of the Flint Trail. The road isn't flat, but there are no major ascents or descents. Along the way, the trees thin out and you catch glimpses of Bagpipe Butte, Elaterite Butte, Island in the Sky, and the La Sal Mountains to the east.

At the top of the Flint Trail you'll find a pullout wide enough for a couple of cars. This is your last chance to turn around easily if road conditions are dangerous. The view of virtually all of Canyonlands is breathtaking from this spot. Take a minute to scope out your route down the ruts and switchbacks. Pay special attention if the road is muddy or snowy. You might run into snow as late as April. If the road is wet, put on tire chains. Mud doesn't make it impossible to descend, but you'll have trouble getting back up the Flint Trail if there is a lot of moisture on the ground.

Zigzag down the switchbacks, letting any mountain bikers in the group go ahead of the vehicles to help in the tricky sections and to avoid dust. The trail is smooth and steep and almost completely non-technical. The only things you'll need are a good set of brakes and the common sense to use them. Resist the macho impulse to completely let it rip until you reach the bottom— you'll live longer.

The road descends more gradually as it takes you out onto Elaterite Basin Road and across the desert toward Maze Overlook. This makes it sound easier than it is. You are still driving through riverbeds, traversing ledges, and making your way over places that seem impassable at first glance.

If you're camping at the Maze Overlook, stick to established campsites. If you're backpacking, drive to the eastern edge of the mesa. There is limited parking here for six to eight cars.

The signed trailhead is northeast of the parking lot (UTM 12 S 0587504/4232373; elevation 5,110). The entire trail down into the Maze is well cairned.

Make sure your pack has as few items hanging off the outside as possible. There are as many as five or six places where you may want to remove your pack and hand it down, either by hand or rope, to get through tight spots. It is definitely Class 4, and a fall in some of these places would be fatal. Because of the trail's exposure, you should pack your backpack so that it doesn't throw you off balance or catch on rocks.

The path begins to the northeast, cutting through a series of White Rim sandstone blocks before morphing into a cairned trail. This trail winds back around to the southeast side of the overlook underneath the top band of vertical rock, and then descends 600 feet in a generally southern direction. You'll primarily be on slickrock during the descent, and navigation will become an exercise in cairn spotting. The descent is airy, but with good judgment you'll be fine.

At 0.8 mile you reach the first spot where you need to lower your packs with a rope. At .96 mile you arrive at the Moki Steps descent, small footholds chipped into the rock that have allowed people to climb up or down steep sections of rock since ancient times. The creation of the Moki Steps is attributed to Native Americans, who have traversed this canyon for thousands of years. At the time of this writing there is a cairn directly above where the steps make their way down the cliff.

There are two sections of Moki Steps here, one right above the other. Continue to follow the cairns down to the canyon floor, lowering packs with rope when necessary.

This drop-in spot for the Maze is the South Fork of Horse Canyon. When you reach the canyon floor, head down wash to the left for 0.6 mile. You will be following the riverbed east, out and around a rock promontory. A large canyon to the left leads down into the main Horse Canyon drainage. But don't go this way. Instead, round the promontory and head to the right.

You'll pass two canyons on your right before arriving at a third, Pictograph Fork. Its name comes from the Harvest Scene, a pictograph panel found within the canyon. As you go up Pictograph Fork, you'll soon arrive at another fork. Stay left and follow the wash to find the pictograph panel. Occasional cairns lead you up the canyon. It isn't necessary to go directly to this panel because you'll pass right by it on the second day.

Locate your campsite beyond view of Maze Overlook.

DAY 2: It's time for the Maze Overlook Loop day hike. Head back out of Pictograph Fork the way you came in, but turn right instead of left at the Horse Canyon drainage. Follow cairns up the wash, and head up the first canyon you come to on the right.

This path is an adventure in route finding. From here on out you must follow the cairns to find your way. After traveling into the canyons you eventually start up a winding path into a narrow side canyon and out onto the rim. Because of the depth of the canyons I was unable to get GPS readings on mileage, but it's approximately 2 miles to the rim. The cairns take you along a winding path for a few hundred yards up under a rim of white Cedar Mesa sandstone.

Once on the rim, you continue following cairns south along a ridge that affords a magnificent view of the Maze. To the left is Jasper Canyon, and you see all the area's major formations—Pete's Mesa, Bagpipe Butte, Chimney Rock, Chocolate Drops, Orange Cliffs. Not until you get to this vantage point do you realize just how large and complex the Maze really is.

The trail, such as it is, leads you across the ridge for 2.9 miles to Chimney Rock (UTM 12 S 0589787/4227061). Hook around Chimney Rock and pick up the trail on the north side. You go farther out across the rim and back down into the Maze. At times, it seems highly improbable that you'll be able to find your way down the steep exposed slopes. Stick to the cairns, which carefully lead you down through passageways and onto shelves and rock piles that take you into the canyon.

A number of different canyons open up at the bottom. Stay in the wash and follow the cairns. You soon come to a fork that appears to circle around a large tower of Cedar Mesa sandstone. Take the right fork and follow it for .25 mile to where a sandy trail leads off the wash to the right. You are now heading into a branch of Pictograph Fork, which leads you through prickly-pear cactus and juniper to the Harvest Scene pictograph panel.

The pictographs (UTM 12 S 0588407/4230731) are on the left wall of the canyon. They are visible from the trail, and the wash dumps you right at the base. This panel contains several hunting and animal scenes, in addition to some ghost-like images. Like the Great Gallery in Horseshoe Canyon, it dates back 8,000 years. Enjoy the pictographs and the shade offered by the cedars. You are now back in Pictograph Fork, where the loop began, and it should be no problem to retrace the route out to Maze Overlook.

RESOURCES

MOUNTAIN BIKE GUIDES
Western Spirit: 1-800-845-2453; www.westernspirit.com/trips/mtb-maze5day/maze5day.html
Rim Tours: 1-800-626-7335; www.rimtours.com/
Escape Adventures: 1-800-596-2953; www.escapeadventures.com/schedule/

USEFUL WEB SITES AND PHONE NUMBERS
National Park Service: 435-719-2313; www.nps.gov/cany (additional information about Horseshoe Canyon rock art can be found online)
Hans Flat Ranger Station: 435-259-2652; 8 AM–4:30 PM
Utah Trails: www.utahtrails.com/maze.html

A LITTLE HISTORY, GEOLOGY, FLORA, AND FAUNA

The earliest settlers in the area, the Archaic People, were hunter-gatherers who lived here 2,000 to 8,000 years ago. From the quality of their drawings, collectively known as Barrier Canyon Style, we know little beyond that they were a surprisingly sophisticated people. Many of the trails around Canyonlands, including the Flint Trail, Big Water–Elaterite Basin Road, and Pictograph Fork were originally Native American routes. Later, around A.D. 1200, the Fremont Indians and Ancestral Puebloans began farming the region. The Fremont Indians generally lived in central Utah, while the Puebloans came up from the south.

For most of the 20th century, this country was the exclusive domain of a few lonely cattlemen, sheepherders, prospectors, and moonshiners. In the 1920s the remote nature of Horseshoe Canyon was shattered by oil exploration. Roads followed, and the canyons became more accessible.

The story goes that a couple of prospectors found oil seeping out of the sandstone in Elaterite Basin near the mouth of Horse Canyon, just a few miles north of Maze Overlook. They sold shares of stock in the Midwest and raised enough capital to start a small drilling project. Despite the fact that most of the Flint Trail was still literally just a trail, they were able to bring their drilling rig in piece by piece using an ingenious cable-winch system. They drilled alone for a year, not realizing that they could never get oil out with the technology they had. The process they used created a minor environmental disaster, but their determination is awe-inspiring.

Canyonlands is a geological feast, but the structure of the Maze is quite simple. The round smooth red, white, and orange walls are Cedar Mesa sandstone. The cap of rock you climb down from at Maze Overlook is White Rim sandstone. The red rock you pass through is Organ Rock shale. The Chocolate Drops across from the Maze have a base of Cedar Mesa sandstone, a narrow spire of Organ Rock shale, and a cap of White Rim sandstone.

The Maze's flora is surprisingly lush, especially during the spring. Deep in the canyons, expect to find an array of plants, including some stout cottonwoods. Tamarisk trees choke many of the small promontories along riverbeds. Prickly pear is numerous and correlates with Native American sites, supposedly the remnants of cultivation. Above the Maze,

Elaterite Basin has a few cottonwoods, although sagebrush is the dominant plant. Up on the Spur, juniper trees dot the landscape. A variety of wildflowers bloom in April, and plants like Mormon tea are found on the upper ridges.

Jasper Canyon, which has been completely closed off to human entry, can be seen from the ridge when you're on the Maze Overlook day hike. Jasper has been closed because it's one of the only areas to escape grazing by domestic livestock. Virtually the entire Colorado Plateau has been heavily grazed for over a century, but Jasper's inaccessibility kept livestock and people out of the area. This isolation has revealed differences—particularly below ground level—between Jasper and nearby canyons that have been trampled.

The plants in Jasper have higher nutrient levels, and there is a notable lack of exotic, non-indigenous plants in the area. It has become a model for how canyon ecosystems should function, providing land managers with better information for setting management goals for millions of other acres. This resource is extremely fragile. A single off-trail footprint can significantly impact the area. Please respect the closure.

The Maze and Horseshoe Canyon area have remnant signs of the archaic people that occupied this region almost continually for roughly 7,500 years. Their pictographs and the occasional ruin attest to their presence. Horseshoe Canyon was once known as Barrier Canyon, so the rock art in the canyon is called Barrier Canyon rock art. Horseshoe Canyon was added to Canyonlands National Park in 1971 because of the abundance of significant rock art.

The Needles

Needles District, Canyonlands National Park

🚶

Taking the Road Less Traveled

Two routes diverge at Elephant Canyon Trailhead in the Needles District of Canyonlands National Park. The first is a 4×4 road that snakes its way to a beautiful graben valley, the Devil's Kitchen, which is surrounded by tall Cedar Mesa sandstone towers and walls. (Grabens are linear collapsed valleys created by the movement of underlying salt layers.) The second route, a trail, snakes its way over, around, and actually

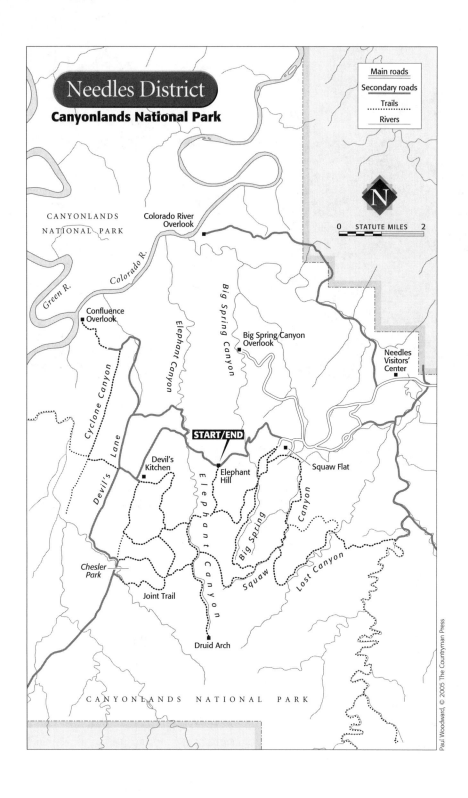

Needles District

Canyonlands National Park

Main roads
Secondary roads
Trails
Rivers

N

0   STATUTE MILES   2

CANYONLANDS
NATIONAL PARK

Colorado River
Overlook

Green R.

Colorado R.

Big Spring Canyon

Elephant Canyon

Confluence
Overlook

Big Spring Canyon
Overlook

Needles
Visitors'
Center

Cyclone Canyon

Devil's Lane

START/END

Devil's
Kitchen

Elephant
Hill

Squaw Flat

Elephant Canyon

Big Spring Canyon

Squaw Canyon

Lost Canyon

Chesler
Park

Joint Trail

Druid Arch

CANYONLANDS   NATIONAL   PARK

Paul Woodward, © 2005 The Countryman Press

through those same jumbled towers to that same graben valley. Most people visiting Devil's Kitchen go by car. But you will take the road less traveled. And that really will make all the difference.

The 18.8-mile, three-day backpack trip outlined here will not only get you to some of the more popular destinations in the area, but also to many places the 4×4s and day-hikers can't reach. You'll see incredibly beautiful but popular graben valleys like Devil's Kitchen and enclosed valleys like Chesler Park. The Joint Trail, a cave-like joint in the pinnacles of the Needles, is a quarter-mile slot canyon just wide enough to walk through with your pack rubbing both walls.

In the Needles you can have the kind of experience most people only dream about. You can wake up in the middle of the night—the day-hikers gone, everyone else asleep—climb to the top of a small pinnacle, and marvel at the moonlight bouncing off a hundred rock fingers that reach up into the starriest sky you've ever seen. This is the payoff for following the road less traveled.

SPORT: Backpacking, hiking

RATING: Moderate to strenuous, depending on the season and the heat

DISTANCE: This is an 18.8-mile loop through several canyons, with side trips to the Confluence Overlook (10.4-mile loop) and to Druid Arch (4 miles out and back).

TIME: Two or three days

GETTING THERE: Head south from Salt Lake City on I-15 toward Las Vegas. Merge onto US 6 at Exit 261 near Spanish Fork, about 50 miles from Salt Lake City. Head east on US 6 through Spanish Fork and the subsequent canyon for approximately 125 miles, until you come to the junction with I-70. Go east on I-70 for 23.2 miles, and then take Exit 180 to continue south on US 191 toward Moab.

Pick up any last minute supplies in Moab and continue south on US 191. Do not turn onto the Needles Overlook Road. Between mileposts 86 and 87, turn right (west) onto UT 211. Follow UT 211 for 34.8 miles to the Needles Visitors' Center, where you'll pick up your backcountry permit. It is 75 miles from Moab to the visitors' center. Continue 2 miles and turn left on the road toward Elephant Hill. Don't turn into the campground itself; continue down the road 2.7 miles to the Elephant Hill Trailhead.

▌▐ TRAIL: The path from Elephant Hill Trailhead in the Needles is well maintained and follows a popular day-hike trail that climbs and traverses sandy packed footpaths and rock floors. You'll cross through gaps between needles and make your way along grassy stretches and meadow valleys. The trail is signed at junctions throughout the Park and is well cairned in difficult sections.

It's impossible to explore the Needles in a weekend, so you'll have to decide which highlights to concentrate on. These include: Chesler Park, a beautiful open meadow surrounded by needle spires; Joint Trail, a section of trail through thin shoulder-width slot canyons; Cyclone Canyon, a 2-mile canyon of uniform orange and white needle spires; Squaw Canyon, slickrock shelves over hills and valleys dotted with trees; Druid Arch, a unique double arch named after the suspected builders of the ancient monument of Stonehenge in England; and Devil's Lane, a graben valley with 100- to 200-foot-high walls that resemble an Old West fort.

Design your loop trail to include the features you would most like to see. There are other areas to consider as well, such as the Confluence Overlook for the Green and Colorado Rivers and canyons like Big Spring, Squaw, and Lost on the other side of the Park.

Please remember to stay on the trail at all times to avoid destroying cryptobiotic soil, a vital building block of the ecosystem here. (See the Introduction for more information on cryptobiotic soil ecosystems.) Ultimately, the success of all plant and animal life in the Needles depends on minimizing impact on these soils.

OPTIONAL ACTIVITIES: Mountain biking the jeep roads is a quick way to enter the Needles and enjoy the towering sandstone minarets. The terrain combines 4×4 jeep trails, loose rock, slickrock, and occasionally sand. (Note the 4×4 roads on the map for the Needles.)

MAXIMUM GROUP SIZE: Backpacking groups are limited to seven.

CAMPING: All campsites in the Needles backcountry are assigned. Work with the ranger to choose sites that best fit the route you wish to take. To minimize impact on this fragile ecosystem, all campsites within the Needles are developed sites. At the entrance to each campsite there's a post with the campsite's name and number. Most campsites are spread far enough apart that you still feel like you're having a wilderness experience. Each site has enough room for several tents.

The Joint Trail

Squaw Flat Campground is a modern developed campground located before Elephant Hill Trailhead. There are 26 sites available on a first-come, first-served basis, bathrooms with flush toilets and running water, fire grates, picnic tables, tent pads, and water (available year-round). Some of the campsites are nestled up to the rocks and sit under mushroom-like caves, so there is a fun ambiance to the place. The maximum is ten people per site, although group sites for 11 or more can be reserved in advance.

SEASON: Late March and April are the busiest months in the Needles, but September and October are the most comfortable months to visit, with daytime temperatures in the 60s and 70s. Be aware that spring weather is very unpredictable. A significant amount of the year's precipitation falls in March and April.

Beginning in May the days start to get pretty hot, with daytime temperatures in the 80s and 90s. Insects begin to hatch at this time too, but I have been there in May when insects were not a problem. Hundred-degree days are common throughout summer, and violent afternoon thunderstorms arrive in July and August.

PERMITS: Backcountry permits are required and must be reserved at least two weeks in advance. They can be picked up at the Needles Visitors' Center from 8 AM–5 PM (www.nps.gov/cany/needles; 435-259-4711).

FEES: The National Park entrance fee is $10 per vehicle, good for seven days.

Backcountry permits run $15.

CLOTHING AND EQUIPMENT: Because springs in the area are unpredictable, water will be your primary concern. Carry in all you need—at least a gallon per person, per day.

Pack your backpack as tight and small as possible to help with your balance on steep slickrock and to make it easier to squeeze through tight gaps between the needles. Bring a good hat and sunscreen. A map of the area will help you find your way along the trails. A fleece jacket will stave off chilly nights in the spring and fall. Long pants and long-sleeved shirts are the best defense against bugs, but remember your repellant if you are traveling during May and June. And don't forget the camera.

SUGGESTED ITINERARY

DAY 1: Arrive at the Needles Visitors' Center and pick up your permit. The first thing you'll probably notice at the Elephant Hill Trailhead is how many other people are there. Relax. Most visitors go just a few hundred yards and then quit. Look up valley and to the right and you'll see the Elephant Hill 4×4 road switchbacking up an impossibly steep incline. The road is extremely rough, even though the Park Service has actually poured cement in a few gaps. It's the real deal, attracting four-wheelers from far and wide.

The trail at Elephant Hill starts as an obvious sandy path that heads up the hill to the south, and it's marked by cairns. Don't get sidetracked on diverging trails. In 0.6 mile you head into the first joint, which spits you out in a park. (A joint is a small slot canyon between two rock walls.) You reach a junction at 1.42 miles. The trail to Squaw Flat Campground heads off to the left, and Chesler Park and Druid Arch are to the right. Follow the trail that matches your itinerary.

Druid Arch is situated high up in the 2-mile-long section of Upper Elephant Canyon, a box canyon with no exit. At 4 miles round trip it makes a nice side hike.

If you're headed toward Elephant Canyon, at 1.7 miles you come to a massive joint—a very thin slot canyon—maybe 24 inches wide. Go down through the slot to get to Elephant Canyon. Climbing out of Elephant Canyon, still on a traditional trail, you cross through gaps between needles and make your way to peaceful Chesler Park.

One of the most popular places in the Needles, Chesler is a meadow surrounded by colorful needles of sandstone. In mid-May it fills with wildflowers that aren't present later in June and July—the common sunflower, blooming prickly pear, pale evening primrose, larkspur, and globemallow.

Between the Joint Trail and Chesler Park there is an eye-popping panoramic vista of the Needles and the Maze. The Joint Trail runs along the southwest side of Chesler Park. The main joint in the Joint Trail is a fabulous shoulder-width canyon that stretches for .25 mile. You come to it as you exit Chesler Park to the west. A stone staircase leads down into the joint. When you come out of the tight slot it opens up a little and trails head off to the side. Don't take these; instead, keep going straight on the sandy footpath down through more cliffs and boulders to a cave that curves off to the right. It's a sanctuary of cairns that hikers have built as they passed through—a cairn museum.

After the main joint, the trail opens onto a sandy footpath that intermittently crosses rock. It eventually descends the rocky hillside and drops into a wash. Cross the wash and follow the trail up the other side.

Where you camp for the night depends on your specific route. Talk with a ranger before your trip to get suggestions for the area you'll be in.

DAY 2: If you're near it you might want to take a side hike to Confluence Overlook, which looks down on the confluence of the Green and Colorado Rivers. Sitting on the edge of the cliff watching the rivers merge 1,000 feet below is worth the effort. Sometimes the Green River really appears green and the Colorado appears red-orange, which makes it look like the University of Miami logo.

Backtrack 1 mile to Cyclone Canyon and turn south on the trail. You're going to be away from the road—finally. You're traveling down a graben valley with almost perfectly vertical, uniform, impenetrable walls. Follow the trail 2 miles south to a junction with the Lower Red Lake Trail. Turn east on the Lower Red Lake Trail, climb a hill into an elevated hollow, and then descend back down into Devil's Lane to reach the road in 1 mile.

The location of your prearranged second night's camp will determine whether you head north or south along Devils Lane. From here, you have only a few miles of trail to follow in order to hook up with Elephant Hill and your car.

RESOURCES

USEFUL WEB SITES AND PHONE NUMBERS

National Park Service Reservations: 435-259-4351; 435-259-4285 (fax); www.nps.gov/cany/reserve.htm; 8 AM–12:30 PM

National Park Service: www.nps.gov/cany/needles

Needles Visitors' Center: 435-259-4711

A LITTLE HISTORY, GEOLOGY, FLORA, AND FAUNA

Obviously the rock formations are the most striking aspect of the Needles area. Made almost entirely of red, white, and orange Cedar Mesa sandstone, the Needles are a geological wonder. As mountains were pushed upward to the east, trapped seawater created a thick layer of salt. After millions of years and more than 30 cycles of advancing and retreating, the ocean fell back to its current western boundary, leaving behind white beach sand that blew into the Canyonlands area and layered itself with red sediment washed down from the mountains.

This happened many times over millions of years and resulted in the striped appearance of the needles. Over the next 250 million years these layers were buried under sedimentary rock. The Colorado and Green Rivers have eroded away the overlying layers through the last 10 million years. Movement by the underlying salt caused these layers to crack, lift, and shift, forming graben valleys. Rainwater and snow further eroded the exposed rock layers, sculpting the rock spires we see today.

Unlike canyons, the grabens (German for "ditches") were not formed by stream erosion but by land slipping down underground faults created by unstable salt layers.

The uniformity of the needles is particularly interesting. Imagine a big layer cake that has been cut into many parallel slices. Now imagine that the bottom layer of every other slice collapses—that's how the needles were formed. The layered rock broke into several parallel fault lines, and then alternating subterranean layers collapsed, creating neat rows of needles and graben valleys. Over time, wind and water have rounded the Cedar Mesa sandstone into natural cathedrals.

Tiny needles of another sort are formed in well-advanced cryptobiotic soil. These innocuous looking dried clumps of black soil have a pretty good hold along many of the trails in the Needles. Without cryptobiotic soil, plant life in the desert wouldn't exist. These soils build up over hundreds of years and provide a fertile place for lichens, mosses, and cyanobacteria (the building blocks of a plant ecosystem) to grow.

When cryptobiotic soils are trampled entire colonies of these building blocks are wiped out in an instant. Plant diversity decreases as a result, leaving the ecosystem vulnerable to fast-spreading invasive plants like cheatgrass, an unwelcome visitor to the valleys of the Needles.

Just south of Chesler Park is a similar meadow called Virginia Park, not shown on any Park Service map. Public access has been banned to allow for scientific research. Because of its inaccessibility to domestic livestock through the years, Virginia Park is a great laboratory for showing how humans and animals affect the desert ecosystem. While it may look like every other park in the Needles, researchers have found that cryptobiotic soils are far better developed here than in other areas, and there's up to 50 percent less cheatgrass present.

Animal life in the Needles is somewhat less developed than in other areas of Canyonlands, largely due to the lack of water. Animals tough enough to brave the dry hot Needles area include rodents, snakes, bighorn sheep, and mule deer. Perhaps the most interesting animal in the Needles area is the Ord's kangaroo rat, which actually gets all the water it needs from plant matter. It spends the day in burrows deep in the soil, sometimes plugging the hole to insulate it from the heat.

Potholes, depressions in the slickrock where water collects after a rain, are actually teeming with life. Tiny organisms with short lifecycles, or ones that can tolerate dehydration, like clams, shrimp, snails, mites, and rotifers, thrive in potholes. Insects and toads use potholes as breeding grounds. Before you stick your foot in a pothole, wet or dry (dehydrated organisms are still present), remember that these micro-ecosystems are incredibly delicate. You could be destroying an example of the most vibrant life-filled habitat in the Needles.

John Wesley Powell was likely the first western explorer to actually see the Needles, on his first great Colorado River journey in 1869. But Denis Julien, a French trapper, made his way to the confluence of the Green and Colorado Rivers as early as 1836. Of course, the Ancestral Puebloans farmed here long before that, and the Archaic People, a hunter-gatherer society, left rock art in the area that dates back thousands of years.

Canyonlands National Park

Canyonlands National Park

 THE WHITE RIM TRAIL

The West's Premier Multi-Day Mountain Bike Adventure

A Native American legend tells of a leader who mourned so deeply over the death of his wife that a route to an eternal world appeared, allowing him to see her again. The route cut through places no one had seen, regions too fantastic for human eyes. The gods who created the trail filled it with water as he passed through, so Man would not

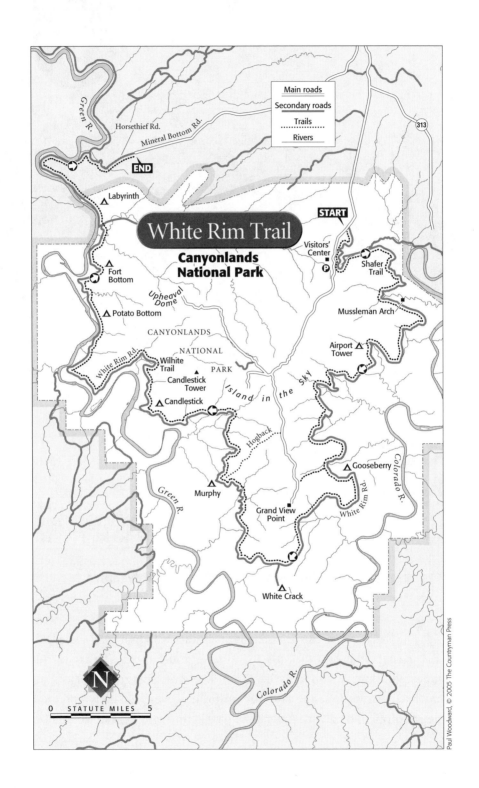

try to follow. Island in the Sky, a huge mesa that dominates the north-eastern third of Canyonlands National Park, is that legendary place.

Located between the Green and Colorado Rivers in southeastern Utah, this 2,000-foot-high mesa sits on shelves of sandstone that rise above the rivers—a land of giant scenery. On a clear day, you can see three different mountain ranges from this mesa: the Abajo Mountains to the south, the Henry Mountains to the southwest, and the La Sal Mountains to the east, their snowy peaks a sharp contrast to the red cliffs and mesas that surround you. The views into the canyons reveal history in the strata of the cliffs, and you can pick out arches and rock forma-tions that have the appearance of wooden shoes, washerwomen, fish fins, and angels.

The 100-mile White Rim Trail, the West's premier multi-day moun-tain bike adventure, loops around the top of Island in the Sky Mesa in the heart of Canyonlands. It has been called the granddaddy of all mountain biking trails, with memorable overlooks of the surrounding country. Regulated by permit, the trail offers a three- to four-day excur-sion that allows your body and mind to escape from the usual routine.

There are no lodges or motels in Canyonlands, no showers, no coin laundries, no restaurants or 7-Elevens. It is a land of sandstone, carved by rivers into a visual history of cliff walls striped in whites and reds, pinks and buffs.

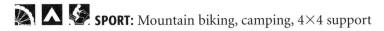 **SPORT:** Mountain biking, camping, 4×4 support

RATING: The trail is moderate during good weather. The most chal-lenging sections are Murphy Hogback, Hardscrabble Hill, and the switchbacks up Horsethief Trail at the end of the ride, but you can walk them if you have to. In inclement weather, parts of the trail become slip-pery, requiring extreme caution. In certain places you will find sand for short distances.

DISTANCE: The trail weaves for approximately 100 miles along spec-tacular buttes and milk-white sandstone columns carved from the red stone. The last 12.9 miles are optional if you're riding with a support vehicle or use a shuttle car.

TIME: Your total time will depend on how vigorously you attack the trail. Some bikers have completed the ride in a singe day, although this approach sacrifices time on the trail with friends, evening contemplations, and hiking. A moderate push brings you around the loop in three or four days.

GETTING THERE: From Salt Lake City, head south on I-15 toward Las Vegas. Merge onto US 6 at Exit 261 about 50 miles south at Spanish Fork. Head east on US 6 for approximately 150 miles, until you come to the junction with I-70. Take I-70 East for 23.2 miles to Exit 180, and then go south on US 191 toward Moab. At 19.3 miles, turn right (west) onto UT 313, which climbs to the top of the Island in the Sky in Canyonlands National Park. The Island in the Sky Visitors' Center is 32 miles from Moab.

You can start the ride from the visitors' center by biking north 1 mile to the Shafer Trail, a dirt-road trailhead. If you leave a shuttle car at the Horsethief Trailhead, where the trail emerges from Mineral Bottom, to help carry out your entire group you can cut off 12.9 uninspiring miles at the end of the loop. We were glad we took this option. (You'll probably be biking with a support vehicle, but if you're with a large group you may still need a separate shuttle vehicle to transport bikes and riders at the end of the trip.)

Be sure to check in at the visitors' center to get your permit before you begin the ride.

TRAIL: One hundred miles long, the trail consists of paved road to and from the visitors center, gravel sections at the beginning and end, and four-wheel-drive dirt road between. The ride begins with a steep descent before paralleling the Green River. Aside from three steep climbs—Murphy Hogback, Hardscrabble Bottom, and Horsethief Hill—the rest of the trail is reasonably level.

The terrain is a combination of loose rock, bedrock, and some sand. The route doesn't require expert skill, but there are a few rough sections

Dinner on the White Rim Trail

and sandy areas. Any rider with a positive attitude who has done one of the intermediate rides in the Moab area will enjoy riding the White Rim Trail.

We'll start the ride near the visitors' center, but it's possible to follow the trail from either direction. A support vehicle is helpful for hauling gear and picking up stragglers who have bonked. No ATVs are allowed.

This adventure is only appropriate for adults and older children who can meet the demands of a moderately difficult trail. I have ridden the trail when six months pregnant by skipping the steep ascents.

Practicing moves on the slickrock

MAXIMUM GROUP SIZE: Regulations allow up to 15 people and three vehicles per permit. Our group included six people and two support vehicles. Pets are not allowed in the backcountry.

CAMPING: The National Park Service requires groups to stay in one of 10 developed campsites along the White Rim Trail. You will select a different campsite for each night when you make your reservation, factoring in the distance you want to travel each day. It's a good idea to divide the mileage equally between your days if you don't want one very long and difficult day.

Camping areas, and their distance from the visitors' center, are listed on the National Park Service web site (www.nps.gov/cany/island/wrim.htm). There is no additional cost for campsites. Pit toilets are provided at each campsite. No potable water is available along the trail, so bring all you'll need for drinking, cooking, and clean up. No fires are allowed.

SEASON: The season runs from March through October, with spring and fall the most pleasant seasons. Summer is exceedingly hot, at times topping 100 degrees. Spring weather is very unpredictable, with a significant amount of the year's precipitation falling in March and April. Violent thunderstorms arrive in July and August.

PERMITS: Permits are required. Make reservations well in advance, especially for spring and fall slots, which fill up early. We made our reservations six months in advance, but you can start making reservations for the following year as early as July. Reservations can be made by mail or fax only. Download the reservation form from the NPS web site (www.nps.gov/cany/reserve.htm) and fax it in (435-259-4285). You must pick up your backcountry permit at the Island in the Sky Visitors' Center. Your reservation is not your permit.

Ask the office staff for suggestions on campsites when making reservations.

FEES: Fees are $30 per group of mountain bikes and 4×4 support vehicles.

CLOTHING AND EQUIPMENT: Bring a selection of clothing to layer. We've been on the trail in the spring when it was 80-plus degrees at midday, but in the evening we couldn't layer enough fleece to keep warm. Pack a waterproof/windproof jacket. If you haven't been on your bike in a while, make sure your shorts are padded—100 miles is a lot of seat time. The trail is rugged, so don't forget your biking gloves. Of course, you also need the basics: helmet, sunglasses, sunscreen, and first-aid kit.

After sweating on a dusty trail all day, you might want to have wet wipes for a daily wipe down, or throw in a portable shower if you have the space and extra water. Include bug repellant if you tackle the ride anytime after the first week in May.

You'll need all the basic camping equipment: tents, pads, sleeping bags, cooking supplies, and flashlights. Since no campfires are allowed, you'll need to bring a stove for cooking. The campsites have no tables, but at some we did find rocks that served as tables and chairs.

Make sure you have extra tubes and tools to maintain your bike on the trail. At a minimum, learn how to fix a flat and repair a broken chain.

A 4×4 support vehicle serves as relief in case of emergency and hauls all camping gear, food, and water. Have riders take turns behind the wheel. Drive carefully, as towing charges in this remote area can be in excess of a thousand dollars. Pack an extra quart of oil and a fan belt for the vehicle just in case, and make sure the spare tire is in good condition.

Bring a gallon of water per person, per day. If you'll be separated from your group of riders during the day, make sure to take plenty of water with you. Your body needs a lot of liquid while biking, and a hot day will take even more out of you. This is not a place to skimp. In summer, if you're not carrying more water than you think is necessary, you don't have enough. On hot days you may need up to three gallons a day. Obviously you're not going to carry all that with you, but plan on refilling at the "sag wagon" from time to time. Take along sport drinks that contain electrolytes to keep your body properly hydrated.

If you plan to filter river water you'll need to bring a container for settling out debris and dirt because the Colorado and Green Rivers are heavily silted. You won't have access to the river on a regular basis.

Bring food with a good mix of carbohydrates for added energy. Since a support vehicle will likely haul your supplies, you won't have concerns about weight; throw in that extra bottle of Chablis. Some chefs have been known to work their gourmet magic on the trail.

SUGGESTED ITINERARY

Make reservations and secure permits at least six months in advance. Because each day will contain something different for each group depending upon their chosen campsites, this itinerary describes the route without breaking it down day by day.

Arrive at the Island in the Sky Visitors' Center (8 AM–4:30 PM) early enough to watch their movie on backcountry etiquette, make all bike adjustments, get your permit, and cover the distance to your first campsite. We arrived early and were on the trail by 9 AM. It's important to allow ample time to complete each day's allotted mileage between the prearranged campsites because leaving the trail or camping outside of campsites is prohibited.

Much of the soil here is cryptobiotic, the essential building block of the desert ecosystem. Leaving designated trails and campsites and trampling this fragile soil can dramatically alter the desert and stunt plant growth.

The route begins 1 mile north of the visitors' center on the Shafer Trail. The bikes and the support vehicle ride on the same road. At 7.8 miles there is a foot-traffic-only path, the Gooseneck Trailhead, which takes you on a half-mile walk to an overlook of the Colorado River. At 9.7 miles Musselman Arch, a natural bridge as wide as a sidewalk, will appear on the left side of the trail. We stopped here and had lunch. The views are unforgettable, and brave hikers can venture across. Don't forget your camera, as you will definitely want to record the amazing scenery.

Memorable overlooks of the Colorado River and tight switchbacks abound. At 17.5 miles the Lathrop Canyon Trail, a side trail you can opt to explore, takes you 4 miles down to the river. The Airport Tower Campsites A & B are found at 18.3 miles, and the Gooseberry Campsites A & B at 28.7 miles.

Sometime during the second day you will probably ride through the southern tip of the Island in the Sky area. Both the Maze and the Needles sections of Canyonlands National Park will come into view. A left turn 37.5 miles from the start takes you out to White Crack Campground (1.5 miles from the main road).

There are fantastic rock formations throughout the ride. At 44.1 miles you come to the infamous Murphy Hogback at 5,200 feet. This is one of three difficult climbs on the route. Three campsites are located on the hogback. Between miles 48 and 52 you will have views of Candlestick Tower and the Green River. Candlestick Campsite is located at 54.3 miles.

At 56.4 miles you come across the Wilhite Trail. The trail is to the right, and a slot canyon washed and eroded by flash floods is to the left. We stopped here and ventured down into the slot canyon, where we found steep drop-offs and indentations filled with water. One member of our party fell into a 4-foot-deep pool of water, barely tossing the video camera out before he got dunked. Slot canyons are beautiful places to explore, but always use caution. Wilhite Trail on the other side of the road is a worthwhile side trip as well.

At mile 61 you come to the turnoff to Queen Anne Bottom, accessible by foot only, which takes you to the Green River. Potato Bottom Campsite A is at 64.1 miles.

The next ascent is Hardscrabble Hill, which leads to Hardscrabble Bottom. A portion of the road is entirely deep sand. If you anticipate the sand and shift into the lowest gear in advance you may be able to keep going. Then again, you may be walking to the next shallow section. Sand provides a great opportunity to practice your steering. Four-wheel-drive support vehicles have no problem making their way along the trail. It's almost as much fun driving as riding. Enjoy the climb, but be careful if it's wet.

The trailhead for Fort Bottom (foot traffic only) is at 66.8 miles. It's a 1-mile trail leading to an Ancestral Puebloan structure, known as the Moki Fort, and a cabin near the river. The cabin was used as a stop for patients being transported downriver to a tuberculosis center. The Hardscrabble campsites are at 68.4 miles. Labyrinth Camp is at 70.4 miles.

Winding down through the red rock cathedrals and church spires, you'll find Moenkopi sandstone carved into gnome-like faces by wind and water, layer after layer of canyon collapsing in on itself. The beauty and intricacies are a testament to the eons of time the rock has endured.

On our third night we stayed at a campsite near the Colorado River. We spent a lovely evening sipping hot chocolate under a full moon, with bats scooting and darting through the night sky. If you're a stargazer, bring your charts. There is a clarity here that you can find only in the backcountry.

The last tough climb is a set of switchbacks that makes its way out of the canyon. You climb nearly 900 feet in this section. It's unnerving to see the dead and decaying carcasses of old jeeps and other vehicles along the road that couldn't quite handle the steep curves. They're from times long past, but it's eerie nonetheless.

We started the climb around noon. When we made it to the top we sat on rocks and ate lunch, retelling stories and congratulating ourselves before loading up the bikes and heading back toward Moab and civilization. Another option is to ride the additional 12.9 miles out on Mineral Bottom Road, which connects to UT 313. (These last 12.9 miles are included in the 100-mile tally.)

RESOURCES

TOURS AND GUIDES
Rim Tours: 1-800-626-7335; 1233 South US 191; $650 per person
Tag-A-Long, Moab: 1-800-453-3292; a 20-mile bike ride from Island in the Sky down to Lathrop Canyon, with a scenic ride back to town on a jet boat; $62.50 per person

BIKE RENTALS
Dreamride: www.dreamride.com
SlickRock Cycles: 1-800-825-9791; www.slickrockcycles.com
Poison Spider Bicycles: 1-800-635-1792; www.poisonspiderbicycles.com/rides.html
Bike Zion: 1-800-4-slikrok; www.bikezion.com
Rim Cyclery: 435-259-5333

4×4 RENTALS
Farabee Jeep Rentals: 1-888-806-5337; www.moabjeeprentals.com
Slickrock Jeep Rentals: 435-259-5678; www.moaboffroad@lasal.net

USEFUL WEB SITES AND PHONE NUMBERS
National Park Service/White Rim Trail: www.nps.gov/cany/island/wrim.htm
National Park Service Reservations: www.nps.gov/cany/reserve.htm
Current weather information: http://nimbo.wrh.noaa.gov/saltlake/; 801-524-5133
Canyonlands National Park (general information): 435-259-7164
Canyonlands Reservation Office: 435-259-4351; 435-259-4285 (fax)

A LITTLE HISTORY, GEOLOGY, FLORA, AND FAUNA

If you sit alone in the desert you can't help but notice the quiet. Your ears will ring with silence. At times you'll hear a scampering lizard brush by a clump of grass or a raven's caw, but more often than not the animals of the desert move quietly around in their world. The mountain lion and bobcat are stealthy and nocturnal; it's a great privilege to actually catch sight of one. The seldom-seen desert bighorn sheep and skittish mule deer eat quietly from the desert black brush and sage. If you are lucky you may even catch sight of a fox, and during the days you can watch hawks float among the cliffs. The air is wonderfully clear and the colors of the cliffs appear to change with the light.

The geology of the White Rim starts with the oldest rock layer on the trail—the Cutler Formation, which dates from 280 million years ago. The La Sal Mountains to the east are the youngest rocks in the area at only 24 million years old. Between these two sections of rock, deserts and seas once moved in and out of the region, mountains were uplifted and eroded, and sediments were deposited, worn, and reconfigured into today's geologic story. For more detailed information about the area's geology you can pick up a small paperback called *A Naturalist's Guide to the White Rim Trail.*

In the 1920s the land on and below the Island in the Sky Mesa was used extensively for winter grazing by local cattle ranchers. By the 1950s the Cold War fueled a boom in uranium prospecting. The uranium ore found in the distinctive greenish layer of the Chinle Formation above the White Rim Plateau attracted prospectors like bees to honey. There are no active mines in the area now, but the White Rim Trail is a legacy from these miners. When the area became a national park in 1963, prospecting was no longer allowed. Avoid entering any old mines you run across, as they may be unstable.

The color, the light, the silence, the wildlife, and the challenge that all form the White Rim Trail experience are indelible. This is a land of contrasts, delicate flowers and hardy plants, hot days and cold windy nights. It is a land that demands respect and gives back memories of the best mountain bike experience in the state. Happy riding.

Water

Lathrop Granary

Colorado River, Canyonlands National Park

 CATARACT CANYON

A Taste of North America's Most Intense Whitewater

Legs gripping the side of the raft and gloved hands wrapped around the rope handles, you ride the rapids in Cataract Canyon like a bucking bronco. It's an experience that leaves you laughing wildly and pumping with adrenaline. With 28 rapids, give or take a few depending on water levels, Cataract is a weekend of floating through the heart of

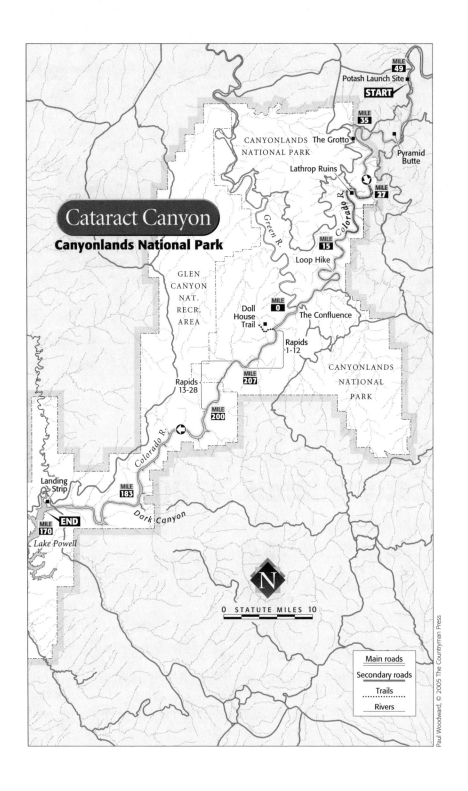

Cataract Canyon
Canyonlands National Park

MILE 49
Potash Launch Site ■
START

MILE 35

CANYONLANDS   The Grotto ■
NATIONAL PARK

Pyramid
Butte ■

Lathrop Ruins ■

MILE 27

CANYONLANDS
NATIONAL PARK

Green R.

Colorado R.

MILE 15

Loop Hike

GLEN
CANYON
NAT.
RECR.
AREA

MILE 0

Doll
House
Trail

The Confluence

Rapids
1–12

Rapids
13–28

MILE 207

MILE 200

Colorado R.

Landing
Strip

MILE 183

END
MILE 170

Lake Powell

Dark Canyon

N

0   STATUTE MILES   10

Main roads
Secondary roads
·········· Trails
Rivers

Paul Woodward, © 2005 The Countryman Press

Canyonlands National Park with Grand Canyon–style Class III to V rapids. Home of the Big Drop, a 30-foot descent in less than a mile, this whitewater on the Colorado River ranks as world-class fun.

There are also side hikes along the way that take you to ancient Indian dwellings, granaries, and art panels. Other hikes lead to grand views or cliffs where you can jump into deep pools of clear spring water. If you have more time and wish to fully explore the day hikes, adding a day or two to your trip is worthwhile. If not, you'll have a full but thrilling weekend.

Cataract Canyon requires technical white-water experience, particularly if you're doing an unguided trip instead of booking a commercial guide service.

SPORT: White-water rafting

RATING: Class III–V whitewater

DISTANCE: 96 river miles

TIME: Three or four days

GETTING THERE: To reach the launch site at Potash Boat Ramp near Moab, head south on I-15 toward Las Vegas from Salt Lake City. Take Exit 261 toward Price/Manti near Spanish Fork about 50 miles from Salt Lake City. Head east on US 6 for approximately 125 miles to the junction with I-70. Take I-70 East for 23.2 miles to Exit 180, which puts you south on US 191 toward Moab and Canyonlands National Park.

Turn right onto Potash Road (UT 279) just before Moab. This road takes you past the potash/salt mines and directly to the boat ramp, 20 miles away. The boat ramp heads down to the left just before the paved road turns to dirt. There is one bathroom and plenty of parking at the site.

The normal take-out is at Hite Marina on Lake Powell, just past the confluence with the Dirty Devil River. This works fine when Lake Powell is full, but when water levels are lower, as they have been for the past few years, the take-out is a ramp (UTM 12 S 0552847/4193531; elevation 3,692) that you come to before you hit Hite Marina on river right. There is a drive for loading and unloading boats, a bathroom, and a parking lot.

If you're going unguided and have parked a shuttle vehicle at Hite Marina you can get back to Moab from the ramp by heading out to UT 95. Follow UT 95 north for 43 miles to Hanksville, where you'll turn right on UT 24. Merge onto I-70 E, go past the town of Green River, and turn right (south) onto US 191, which goes right through Moab.

If you'd rather catch a plane back to Moab, the cost is reasonable ($80 to $100) and the aerial view of southern Utah and Canyonlands is unbeatable. To reach the airstrip, take a right as you come out of the launch site, cross the Dirty Devil River, and look for the airstrip on the right after a five-minute drive. You'll see a sign for AIRCRAFT LANDING and an orange windsock on a tall pole (UTM 12 S 0554853/4194269; elevation 3,917).

In the Moab area, Redtail Aviation and Slickrock Air Guides provide this service, as well as Green River Aviation out of the city of Green River.

RIVER: It's 49 miles from the launch at Potash Boat Ramp on the Colorado River to the confluence with the Green River. The first rapids come 4 miles after this confluence. There are approximately 28 rapids in all, but their location and severity depend upon water levels—how many cubic feet per second (cfs) the river is running.

The first day is entirely flat water, and you tackle the rapids on days two and three. If there is a fourth day, it will cover the flat water on the way to the take-out at Lake Powell's Hite Marina. On three-day trips, the final flat water is covered late on the third day.

As with all river trips, the flow of water determines many things. Campsite availability changes with water level, as some camps won't be accessible at high water. When the river is running at a high of 50,000 cfs it covers a slightly different path than at 5,000 cfs, and obviously the rapids will be different animals. Some areas hold rapids in high water, some in low water. Some side canyons are less accessible in high water, and boat tie-up areas vary.

The accumulation of silt during high water also changes the body of the river, and when low water is pulling the silt down toward Lake Powell

Cataract Canyon

it often uncovers rocks within the riverbed that might have been covered for many years. To experience this river is to explore its ever-changing nature.

 **MAXIMUM GROUP SIZE:** 40

CAMPING: Down to the confluence of the Green and Colorado Rivers, campsites are taken on a first-come, first-served, find-a-sandy-beach basis. A mile and a half past the confluence you'll see a small campsite sign-in box found just under the Cataract Canyon Warning sign on river right. The box is small, 18 x 12 inches, and has sign-up

Camping on the Colorado River

sheets that show which campsites are still available downriver. Gauge the number of miles you plan to cover each day and sign up for the sites that best fit your schedule.

Please remember that even the smallest crumb or scrap of food left at a campsite will attract ants and rodents. All food, trash, and solid waste must be carried out. You are responsible for providing your own river toilet system, which can be rented from a variety of rafting companies. It is standard river-running practice to urinate in the river and defecate in the portable toilet system. (As this is a high-traffic area, urinating on dry ground would quickly leave the banks smelling like a sewage plant.) Leave spotless campsites and river trails and always be aware of your impact on this delicate area.

SEASON: The season runs from April 15 to October 15. High water in May and early June creates the biggest rapids. The water is often cold enough that wetsuits are a good idea during the early months. In July and August the river runs lower, rapids become less extreme, and the sun gets hotter. Bugs are usually worse after a high-water season, when standing pools are left along the banks.

PERMITS: To run Cataract Canyon you must go with an authorized river-running guide who has obtained the required permits or obtain your own. Call 435-259-7164, visit the Canyonlands National Park web site at www.canyonlands.national-park.com/camping.htm#permit, or email canres@nps.gov with permit questions. Permits can only be obtained by mail or fax (435-259-4285). They become available January 1 for the following year.

FEES: For private parties, there is a nonrefundable reservation fee of $30. If you're going on a guided trip, most companies charge from $600 to $1000. Call for exact prices. Shuttle flights are $80 to $100.

CLOTHING AND EQUIPMENT: To complete Cataract Canyon in a three-day weekend you will need a boat equipped with a motor. I have used a mini J-rig (pontoon boat) with a motor, which made it possible to do the almost 100 river miles and plenty of side hikes in four days. This boat fits up to eight people and has ample room for food and kitchen supplies, so cooking on the river can be as fancy as you like.

Sunscreen, sunglasses, a wide-brimmed hat with a chin strap, a long-sleeved white shirt, and sarong are all must-haves, as is bug repellant (especially after high water), plenty to drink, and a river toilet for hauling out all human waste. A tent, sleeping pad and bag, pillow, a good book, and a headlamp are obvious camping items, but also bring a jacket for when the evenings cool down, toiletries and a first-aid kit, and a day-pack for hiking excursions.

Personal flotation devices (PFDs) are mandatory below the confluence of the Green and Colorado Rivers. Many river-runners bring a pair of gloves to help them hold onto the ropes while going over rapids, as well as good water sandals that will hold up on any trails you want to explore. Definitely take a camera, and if you have a GPS the coordinates below will help you pinpoint places of interest.

Be prepared with enough garbage and resealable bags to carry out all trash. Dry bags will keep your belongings dry, and coolers with block ice will give you the luxury of a cold drink despite the desert sun. A canopy on your boat offers great protection from the sun during flat-water days. Make sure you have enough drinking water and sport drinks to keep yourself well hydrated, which will stave off heat exhaustion and the headaches that come with it.

SUGGESTED ITINERARY

DAY 1: The day starts around 8 AM with a scenic drive to the Potash Launch Ramp about 20 miles from Moab. The ramp is at river mile 49, with the confluence downstream being river mile 0. This is a calm day of drifting through the magnificent scenic canyon carved by the Colorado River, with an optional set of side hikes.

At river mile 34, on river right, is the Grotto. The award-winning Moab Music Festival uses this open amphitheater sandstone cave each year. It is one of eight locations in the area where artists from around the country come to perform classical chamber music, traditional music, vocals, works of living composers, and jazz.

Today you have the chance to venture to the Lathrop Canyon ruins on river left between river miles 24 and 23 (UTM 12 S 0607497/4247313; elevation 3,930). A sand stairway leads up the bank, taking you the first 100 feet on a footpath that makes its way under a canopy of tamarisk and cedar. At times this area has the hottest temperatures in the country, so take water with you even though the hike to the granary and pictographs is less than a mile.

The granary is located 0.27 mile along the sandy footpath (UTM 12 S 0607384/4247200; elevation 3,921). Ancient handprints can be seen southeast of the granary, and you'll pass a triptych of pictographs along the north-facing cliff on the way in. Just north of the main granary, a short trail leads you to a second granary. These two granaries and two pictograph panels are easily found along the trail, but the area is also rumored to hold a number of ancient cliff dwellings and art sites. Round trip, the hike is just over a half mile. Lathrop Canyon is also the last place for jeep road access to the river.

At river mile 11 you come to what is called the Loop Hike. The river meanders around an anticline and sweeps back around on the other side of the "loop" at river mile 7. Everyone but the person manning the boat can hop out and make their way up and over the cliff band on river left (UTM 12 S 06034741/4233485; elevation 3,891), meeting the raft on the other side. The Loop Hike is 0.78 mile and takes about 40 minutes. The trail can be done by old and young alike, but be smart and careful.

You need to cover 30 to 40 river miles on day one.

DAY 2: Today you hit the confluence, and then sign in at the campsite registration box (UTM 12 S 0595947/4226141; elevation 3,982) 1.5 miles downstream under the Cataract Canyon Warning sign. Life jackets are required below the confluence.

Just before your first taste of rapids you come to the Doll House hike. Located on river right at mile 213, the well-established trail starts at the base of the tallest cottonwood trees, which have three downed logs at their base (UTM 12 S 0593557/4223786; elevation 3,842). The views and granaries are what draw people to the Doll House, a collection of orange and white hoodoos, or pinnacles, at the top of the canyon. Plan on four hours to complete the trek up and back.

Rapids 1 and 2 are between river miles 213 and 212. These rapids are formidable in high water, dropping to Class III in low water. The first 10 rapids fall within a 5-mile stretch. Rapid 7 is big in high water, and rapid 10 is big in low water. At river mile 205, rapid 13 begins a stretch called Mile-Long Rapids. In this mile you hit rapids 13 through 18. Enjoy the ride. Rapid 19 is big in high water.

Stop for the night at the campsite you registered for at the sign-in box below the confluence.

DAY 3: Rapids 21 through 23 are known as the Big Drop Rapids and rank Class IV, even at low water. These rapids are found between river miles 203 and 202. On river right, from river mile 203.5 to 202.5, there are a number of inscriptions made in the rock walls by exploring parties who passed through from 1891 to 1940. You finish the last few rapids in the next 2 miles.

After that, the water is calm and flat. Motor down to Dark Canyon on river left at mile 183 (UTM 12 S 0569891/4194592; elevation 3,619). When Lake Powell is full, the mouth of Dark Canyon is filled with water. But thanks to the low water over the past five years, the mouth currently has a sandy beach on which you can pull up and tie your boat.

The hike up and back in Dark Canyon takes around four hours. It starts with a half-mile dry trail through some Russian thistle bush, and then turns into a trickle that turns into a stream that eventually leads to cliffs with deep pools beneath, which you can jump into. The water is clear and cool, and this is the highlight hike of Cataract Canyon. If you do only one day hike, make it this one.

There's nothing but flat water the rest of the way to the take-out near river mile 169.

RESOURCES

TOURS AND GUIDES

Tag-a-Long Expeditions: 1-800-453-3292; www.tagalong.com

Adventure-Bound River Expeditions (Grand Junction, Colorado): 1-800-423-4668; www.raft-colorado.com

USEFUL WEB SITES AND PHONE NUMBERS

Green River Aviation Flight Service: 1-877-597-5479; www.greenriveraviation.com

Slickrock Air Guides (Moab airport): 435-259-6216

Redtail Aviation (Moab airport): 1-800-842-9251

Canyonlands National Park, River District: 435-259-7164; www.nps.gov/cany

Tex's Riverways in Moab, Utah (toilet rentals): 435-259-5101; www.texsriverways.com

Colorado Basin River Forecast Center (to check current cfs): www.cbrfc.noaa.gov

A LITTLE HISTORY, GEOLOGY, FLORA, AND FAUNA

In 1869 John Wesley Powell and his crew explored Cataract Canyon. Their notes tell of huge rapids and falls more difficult than any they had run into previously; thus the name Cataract Canyon. Complicated portages over great angular blocks, talus strewn along the channel, dangerous chutes and whirlpools, great waves, and rushing breakers— for Powell and his men, Cataract Canyon was every bit a white-water adventure.

They weren't the first white men to make their way through this remote and beautiful land, though. In 1836 a French trapper named Denis Julien recorded the first trip along the river. The inscription he left is between river miles 185 and 186, but it's now submerged under Lake Powell.

In 1855 the Mormons, the first group to settle around Moab, were forced out of the area by hostile Native Americans after only five months. Twenty years would pass before permanent settlement. Livestock was the primary source of income until the uranium boom exploded on the scene. During the 1950s, uranium mining created speedy population growth in the Moab area. This boom ended in the 1970s and Moab's population dwindled, only to rise again with the development of recreational opportunities.

Over the years the wildlife of the area has maintained its balance. If you watch closely, you may see beaver, the occasional river otter, bighorn sheep, lizards of all types, snakes, tadpoles, frogs, rodents, blue herons, peregrine falcons, red-tailed hawks, mule deer, and geese.

As you head toward the Potash Launch Site you'll pass the potash/salt mine for which the area is named. Established in the 1960s by Texasgulf Sulphur, this mine—along with the uranium boom—made Moab a place of note. The potash was extracted by injecting river water underground until the water was saturated with the salts. It was then brought to the surface, where it was left to evaporate. The leftover potassium chloride crystals were collected and stripped of the chloride so the remaining soluble potassium could be used in fertilizers.

Today, much of the mining is for the salt that was laid down over millions of years by the evaporation of shallow seas. There are thousands of feet of these salt beds in the Canyonlands area, and they are responsible for shaping much of the land.

The canyons of Canyonlands National Park are littered with proof of past civilizations. Some of the granaries and art sites can be seen on the side hikes I've mentioned for this river trip, but it's rumored that there are many more around. Granaries are places where food, or possibly seeds, was stored to keep it from the rodents or perhaps out of direct sunlight. It has also been suggested that these storage facilities were placed high on canyon walls in an attempt to keep them from other people.

At any rate, many of the remains show the indentations of ancient fingers that secured the slabs of rock with river mud. And many are well preserved because the desert climate slows decomposition. The ghosts of people gone before add to the mystery and awe of a trip through Cataract Canyon.

Antelope Island

Antelope Island State Park

Island Recreation on One of the World's Saltiest Bodies of Water

Antelope Island is the largest island in the Great Salt Lake. It is also the only place of its kind, a 28,000-acre island sitting in the middle of the saltiest body of water in the world after the Dead Sea. A refuge for millions of migrating shorebirds, the island may be best known for its wildlife viewing. Birds make extensive use of the lake and surrounding wetlands as a stopover on their journeys north and south each year. It's a birdwatcher's paradise.

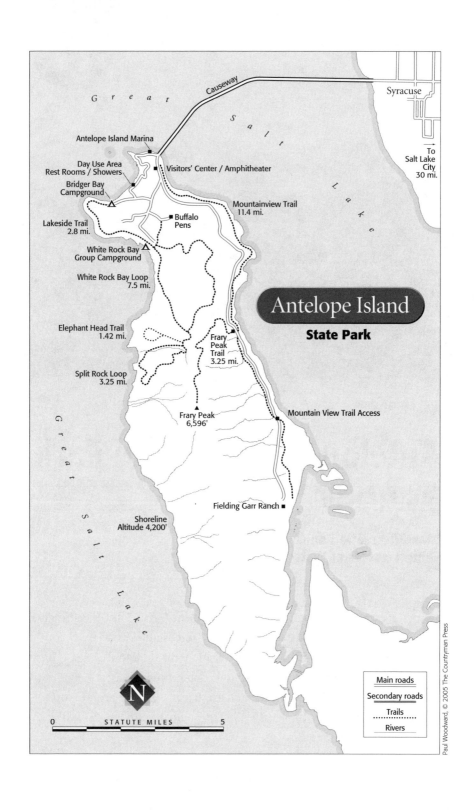

Great Salt Lake

Causeway

Syracuse

To
Salt Lake
City
30 mi.

Antelope Island Marina

Day Use Area
Rest Rooms / Showers

Visitors' Center / Amphitheater

Bridger Bay
Campground

Mountainview Trail
11.4 mi.

Lakeside Trail
2.8 mi.

Buffalo
Pens

White Rock Bay
Group Campground

White Rock Bay Loop
7.5 mi.

Elephant Head Trail
1.42 mi.

Frary
Peak
Trail
3.25 mi.

Great Salt Lake

Split Rock Loop
3.25 mi.

Frary Peak
6,596'

Mountain View Trail Access

Fielding Garr Ranch

Shoreline
Altitude 4,200'

Antelope Island
State Park

N

| 0 | STATUTE MILES | 5 |

Main roads
Secondary roads
Trails
Rivers

Paul Woodward, © 2005 The Countryman Press

Hiking to Frary Peak

This is the lesser-known Utah. In the words of Terry Tempest Williams, "There is no place to hide and so we are found." An island of shores and marshland, grassland and sagebrush, springs and rocky peaks, it is home to waterfowl, bison, mule deer, eagles, raptors, bighorn sheep, and a host of other mammals. We even found frog eggs in an inland pool created by one of the 40 freshwater springs on the island. It's a place where the moon seems bigger, where the colors in the sunrise and sunset have nothing to compete with. It's just 7.2 miles from a million other people, and yet while you're there you feel hidden and yet found.

You can reach this desert island via a paved causeway. Once there, you have access to 35 miles of non-motorized trails that allow visitors to discover the island and its wildlife by hiking or mountain biking.

SPORT: Mountain biking, road biking, kayak touring, camping, saltwater bathing, wildlife viewing

RATING: Suggested trails are moderate. Kayaking is strenuous if you tackle a significant distance, such as rounding the entire island in a day.

DISTANCE: There are 35 miles of trails, with nine hiking/mountain biking routes and approximately 15 miles of road for road biking. The perimeter of Antelope Island covers 39 miles. The Great Salt Lake encompasses 1,700 square miles with a maximum depth of 33 feet.

TIME: A trip here can be as long or as short as you want. Each day provides an opportunity for a new trail or activity.

GETTING THERE: You can reach Antelope Island via a 7.2-mile causeway accessed from Exit 335 off I-15 in Syracuse a few miles north of Salt Lake City. Turn west off the exit and simply follow the road, which takes you directly to the causeway.

TRAIL: Featured Trail. The Frary Peak Trail is a hiking-only path to the highest point on the island at 6,596 feet, with a moderate rating due to steepness and terrain. It covers 6.5 miles out and back. You'll enjoy a wonderful view of the lake, the Wasatch Range, the desert to the west, and the island's campsites, trails, rocky peaks, and grasslands. You may see buffalo and an occasional deer as well.

Featured Road Bike Route. If you're a road biker, you might want to try the 11.4-mile road that follows Mountain View Trail. Starting at the north corner of the island, the road hugs the east shoreline to the Fielding Garr Ranch. It's a pleasant 22.8-mile round-trip ride, and a tour of the ranch is a good way to break up the day.

Featured Kayak Route. Kayakers can launch their craft at the Antelope Island Marina on the northern tip of the island and paddle along the shoreline. On low-water years the island has a swampy mudflat section at the south end. No camping is allowed outside the campground, so all paddle trips must be completed within a day. As long as

An island rookery in Great Salt Lake

you come at the right time of year and are not paddling through hordes of brine flies, the trip is pleasant and salty.

MAXIMUM GROUP SIZE: Group size is only regulated at campgrounds. Two vehicles and up to eight people and two tents are allowed at each campsite.

CAMPING: Camping is allowed in designated campgrounds only. Bridger Bay Campground has 26 primitive campsites, and White Rock Bay Group Campground has five primitive group sites available through reservation only. Both campgrounds have pit toilets. There is no running water at the campsites, but there is a water spigot near the visitors' center where you can fill jugs. Fire pits and grills are available at each site, and there is a dump station on the island for recreational vehicles.

The campgrounds are desert, with sagebrush and no shade. As you walk in the oolitic sand—perfectly round grains formed from layers of calcium carbonate—you sink to your ankles. The sand is so deep and conforming that you don't even need a sleeping pad. Campsites are $10 a night, but if you call and make a reservation you will be charged an additional $7. Reservations are recommended for weekends, but I have been here on a June weekend when plenty of campsites were available.

Day-use facilities on the island include a sandy beach, indoor and outdoor shower facilities, a pavilion, picnic areas, and modern rest rooms.

SEASON: Timing is crucial at Antelope Island if you don't want to be barraged by the smell of rotting brine fly pupae or overrun by the swarms of annoying but harmless mature flies. April, May, early June, and September are the best months to visit. July and August are hot and miserable due to the flies and the smell. October is the season for harvesting brine shrimp, and planes and boats descend upon the lake in the true spirit of a multimillion-dollar capitalist industry. Fielding Garr Ranch is open year-round.

PERMITS: No permits are necessary.

FEES: The day-use fee is $8 per vehicle, and biking or walking into the park runs $4. There is a causeway fee of $2, and camping sets you back $10.

CLOTHING AND EQUIPMENT: Beyond your usual camping and sporting gear, I recommend bringing bug repellant, sunscreen, good hiking shoes, and a camera. If you're camping you may want to set up some sort of portable shade.

Bring containers for carrying your own water and plenty of lotion for soothing your skin. The high salinity levels have a tendency to irritate sensitive skin, so don't shave right before getting in the water. There are freshwater showers at the day-use areas for washing off after a dip in the water. Rinse children well, as they often have more sensitive skin. My son's legs stung after wading on the beach.

SUGGESTED ITINERARY

DAY 1: Arrive, set up camp, stop at the visitors' center to learn more about the island, and pick up current maps and information. After you've gotten a feel for the place, choose your trails. These range from easy to moderate, so you can customize your day.

Try a mountain bike ride on one of the trails, such as the Lakeside Trail, which gives you exposure to the unique geology of the island. Trails along the lakeshore provide views of shorebirds and wetlands. White Rock Bay Loop is a moderate trail with long ascents and descents that provide more of a challenge. There are good wildlife-viewing opportunities along this trail as well.

If you prefer to road bike, you can do laps on roads that are used for various races and group rides through the year. One suggested route would be to take the road that winds down the east side of the island for 11.4 miles to the Fielding Garr Ranch. There's usually a breeze off the water, and you'll have great views of the lake and perhaps bison and waterfowl.

Built in 1848, Fielding Garr Ranch is the oldest Anglo settlement in Utah. It's located at Garr Springs, one of the strongest natural springs on the island. You can take a free tour of the original structures or hike through nearby wetlands.

DAY 2: Rise early and head to the marina so you can watch the sun rise over the Wasatch Range as you paddle your kayak across the lake. The sunsets and moonrises on the island were captivating when I was there—the unobstructed sky, the reflections on the water, the light clean and rich.

Paddle along the east side of the island, heading south from the marina. Take lunch and plenty of water. There are no trails or developments around the southern tip of the island, but you'll have plenty of opportunities for bird- and wildlife watching. No fish live in Great Salt Lake due to the high saline levels, and rangers on the island caution against putting your face in the water because the salt content may choke you.

Sailboats, rafts, canoes, kayaks, jet skis, and motorboats are all allowed on the lake, but it is seldom crowded and non-motorized boats are the norm.

DAY 3: Frary Peak Trail is a hiking-only trail with the best views and photography opportunities on the island. Hike morning or evening for the best light and the most comfortable temperatures.

The trailhead is located approximately 5 miles down the road along the east shore. Roads and trails on the island are all well marked and easy to follow. There is plenty of parking at the trail-head. Take water and your camera. Expansive views of the island and the lake, other islands, and the surrounding landscape make this hike worth every step. The trail is closed April 1 through May 31 for bighorn sheep lambing season.

RESOURCES

BIKE AND KAYAK RENTALS

REI: 801-486-2100; touring kayak rentals
Canyon Sports LTD: 1-800-482-4754; mountain and road bike rentals
Holiday Expeditions: 1-800-624-6323; kayak rentals
Wasatch Touring: 801-359-9361; bike and kayak rentals

USEFUL WEB SITES AND PHONE NUMBERS

Camping Reservations: 1-800-322-3770

State Parks Information: www.stateparks.utah.gov
Antelope Island Park Headquarters: 801-773-2941

A LITTLE HISTORY, GEOLOGY, FLORA, AND FAUNA

Home to a herd of at least 500 bison, 160,000 California gulls, and a stopover for millions of migrating waterfowl, this desert island is teeming with life, but not in the same ways one would usually imagine. The beach looks like any other until you realize that only algae, brine flies, and brine shrimp can withstand the mineral levels in the water; however, these three life forms thrive. The brine shrimp and brine flies feast on the algae, while the birds enjoy both the flies and the shrimp. The lake is the largest supplier of brine shrimp in the world.

Great Salt Lake is the largest U.S. lake west of the Mississippi River and the fourth largest terminal lake (no outlet) in the world. A remnant of Lake Bonneville, a prehistoric freshwater lake that was 10 times larger than the Great Salt Lake during the last ice age, the current lake is about 75 miles long, 28 miles wide, and covers 1,700 square miles. It has a maximum depth of about 35 feet and is typically three to five times saltier than the world's oceans. Four major rivers drain into the lake each year, carrying 2.2 million tons of minerals. Because there is no outlet, evaporation and the minerals combine to create the high saline level.

Artifacts on Antelope Island reveal more than 6,000 years of human habitation. Native Americans showed Jim Bridger the island in 1824, and John C. Fremont and Kit Carson made the first Anglo exploration of the island in 1845. They named the island after watching the abundant antelope graze the grasslands.

In 1847 Mormon pioneers began exploring the island, and less than a year later they had established the first permanent structure, a small log cabin. A man named Garr was assigned by the Mormon Church to establish a ranch for the management of church tithing herds, and thus Fielding Garr Ranch was created. In 1856 the church transported three thousand head of horses and livestock to the island, and between 1872 and 1877 over seven thousand sheep were brought in.

The island was eventually purchased by a private businessman named John Dooly. He introduced bison to the island in 1893, and ranching operations continued through several owners. The ranch functioned as part of one of the prominent cattle operations in Utah until the island became a state park in 1981. Today you can still tour the shearing barn, the springhouse, bunkhouse, commissary, and main living quarters. The freshwater springs on the island provide a source of water for wildlife, ranching herds, and of course the people who have lived here through the centuries.

The American bison herd on the island currently ranges around 500 to 700 head. A certain number are sold each year to keep the herd manageable. The yearly roundup is held in October. Antelope Island is also home to bobcats, coyotes, reptiles, shorebirds, waterfowl, eagles, mule deer, and bighorn sheep.

The southern two-thirds of the island contain some of the oldest rock found anywhere in North America. The Farmington Canyon Complex dates to 2.7 billion years ago, older than rocks found at the bottom of the Grand Canyon. The rock on the northern third of the island dates back 550 million years and was deposited in a marine environment.

Nearly 80 percent of Utah's wetlands surround the Great Salt Lake, making it one of the most important migratory points in North America. The area hosts 250 bird species each year. Half of the eight islands on the lake are rookeries, and public access is not allowed.

A beach camp on Lake Powell

Lake Powell

LABYRINTH, FACE, AND
WEST CANYONS

Cruising the Waters of the Most Scenic
Man-Made Lake in America

Lake Powell, with a horizon of dramatic color and shape that stretches between aqua-blue water and baby-blue sky, is an inland kayaking dream. Because the canyons are narrow enough that motorboats must go elsewhere, you leave the crowds behind and find serenity. To top it off, these narrow canyons often end with scenic hikes into slot canyons. And with water levels currently at just 42 percent of the high

141

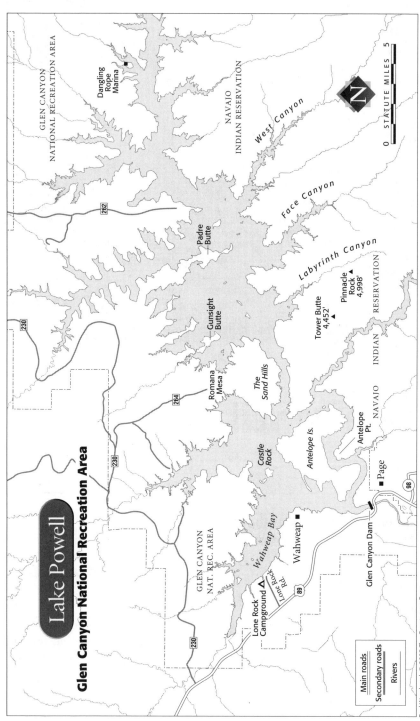

Lake Powell

Glen Canyon National Recreation Area

GLEN CANYON NATIONAL RECREATION AREA

Dangling Rope Marina ■

NAVAJO INDIAN RESERVATION

West Canyon

262

Padre Butte

Face Canyon

Labyrinth Canyon

Pinnacle Rock ▲ 4,998'

Gunsight Butte

Tower Butte 4,452' ▲

230

The Sand Hills

NAVAJO INDIAN RESERVATION

Romana Mesa

264

Antelope Is.

Antelope Pt.

Castle Rock

230

Page ■

98

Wahweap Bay

Wahweap ■

GLEN CANYON NAT. REC. AREA

Glen Canyon Dam

230

Lone Rock Campground ▲

Lone Rock Rd.

89

Main roads
Secondary roads
Rivers

N

0 STATUTE MILES 5

Paul Woodward, © 2005 The Countryman Press

Paddling into a slot canyon

water mark, the walls are higher and the slot canyons deeper and more of Glen Canyon is accessible for exploration. Lake Powell is surrounded by some of the most magnificent scenery in the world. Combine that with the lake's clear deep waters, and there's no other place like it.

The second largest reservoir in the country, Lake Powell has 96 canyons. Not all of these provide sandy beaches to camp on, narrow slots to hike through, or launch sites within reasonable proximity for kayak exploration, but some do combine all these elements. Labyrinth, Face, and West Canyons in particular rank among the best canyons for kayak touring and slot-canyon hiking.

Because of the high cliff walls there are limited launch sites on the lake; most of the reasonably accessible spots are established marinas. You'll have to either paddle to your destination or arrange a motorboat shuttle to the canyon of your choice. But it's worth the trouble, as these three canyons offer you a wonderful chance to enjoy solitude and a great adventure.

 SPORT: Kayak touring

 RATING: Moderate to strenuous, depending on whether you paddle from the marina or take a shuttle and/or guide. Weather will also affect the difficulty level.

DISTANCE: It's 18.6 miles from Wahweap Marina to the mouth of Labyrinth Canyon. How much time you have available will determine whether you paddle or take a shuttle boat. It's a half-day paddle up Labyrinth Canyon (one hour each way) and a full day up West Canyon (approximately 2.5 hours each way) and Face Canyon (approximately two hours each way)

TIME: Three days

GETTING THERE: From Salt Lake City, head south on I-15 toward Las Vegas for 213 miles. At Exit 95, take a left onto UT 20 for 20.6 miles to

US 89. Turn right (south) onto US 89 for 10 miles and then turn left onto East Center Street/US 89 and continue on US 89 for 67.5 miles. Then make another left turn to stay on US 89 for an additional 70 miles. The road takes you right past Wahweap Marina and on to Page, Arizona.

LAKE: The water at Lake Powell is a lovely blue-green. The lake usually sports calm, pleasant paddling waters, but the open water in the main channel can be choppy when you're fighting the motorboat crowd or a stiff wind.

The canyons suggested for this adventure—Labyrinth, Face, and West—are too narrow for motorboats to enter. Assuming there's no wind, this gives you the luxury of pristine, calm water. If you're paddling to one of these canyons from a major launch point you must cross open water, where there can be significant motorboat traffic.

The slot canyons are still a bit wet from years of being submerged below Lake Powell, so watch out for quicksand. I recommend wearing shoes when hiking up the slot canyons to protect your feet from little thorns left in the sand by tumbleweeds. The slot canyons are often shady and pleasant, with occasional waterfalls and seeps. All three of the canyons discussed here end with slot-canyon hikes.

Wahweap Marina straddles the Utah/Arizona border and has short- and long-term parking, bathrooms, showers, laundry, campgrounds, and an array of other public services.

If you have more time—and strong arms—the Escalante Arm of Lake Powell farther to the north is filled with some of the most beautiful side canyons in the Glen Canyon area. Fishing is also popular year-round on the lake. Striped bass, large and smallmouth bass, crappie, catfish, and carp are all present.

MAXIMUM GROUP SIZE: There are no group limits in the Glen Canyon National Recreation Area. Guide services usually limit groups to around 12.

CAMPING: Campsites on the lake vary with water level, but sandy beaches work best. Be forewarned that many of the canyons sport stark

Leaving open water on the lake

cliff walls with no beaches, so if you explore canyons beyond the ones suggested here be sure you locate a good beach before nightfall.

National Park Service regulations require that you provide your own toilet system while on the lake, and everyone must carry out all their own trash. Because desert soil lacks the fungi and bacteria to efficiently decompose buried organic material, don't bury even small items like apple cores or cigarette butts. Everything must be bagged and hauled out. Illegal dumping should be reported to the National Park Service. There are eight floating toilet/dump pump-out stations on the lake. Refer to a current map of Lake Powell to locate where these may be at any given time.

The mouth of Labyrinth Canyon has a perfect sandy beach for camping (UTM 12 S 0471492/4096586; elevation 3,576). The mouth of West Canyon also has a good sandy beach, and Face has a combination of slickrock and sand on the west side of the canyon mouth.

RV parks and a concessionaire-operated campground can be found at the Wahweap Marina. Reserve a spot when you first arrive at the marina, as sites are filled on a first-come, first-served basis. The campsites do not have hook-ups.

SEASON: Spring is pleasant—not too hot, not too crowded—although it is windy at times. Summer is great because the water reaches temperatures of 80 degrees. Even when the sun beats down on 100-degree days, you can always cool off with a dip in the lake.

Summer is also high season for motorboats. Paddling in the open waters is more appealing in spring and late fall. I have paddled here in April and October, and though the lake is less crowded, spring was windy and fall chilly during those visits. Most paddlers consider fall the most pleasant and uncrowded time of year. The lake is accessible in winter, but there may be snow.

PERMITS: Not required.

FEES: There is an entry fee to the Glen Canyon Recreation Area, which is managed by the National Park Service. It's the usual National Park fee schedule. A seven-day entrance permit costs $10 per vehicle, and it's another $10 per motorized boat, with each additional boat costing $4. The price for a shuttle varies with the individual provider. No fees for kayaks.

CLOTHING AND EQUIPMENT: In spring and fall, bring a warm hat, gloves, and a good jacket. During warmer weather, be sure to throw in the sunscreen, a hat, and your sunglasses. There are no water taps on the beaches, so bring water or a filtering system. Water shoes/sandals and a sarong are always staples on the water. Bring firewood and a fire pan if you wish to enjoy chats of paddling adventures around a campfire. And you will most definitely want your camera. We brought a satellite radio that provided morning and evening music.

Though the beaches are sandy and often soft, a good sleeping pad will insulate you from cold that seeps from the ground. I have had a few uncomfortable nights on cold sand during October and April.

Take dry bags to protect your belongings, especially on day hikes that require trekking through water. You'll need all your normal camping and paddling equipment, including life jackets. Don't forget the required portable toilet systems, along with bags to haul garbage out. If you go on a guided trip, food, firewood, and gear will likely be taken care of.

SUGGESTED ITINERARY

DAY 1: At Wahweap, load your kayaks on the shuttle boat that will take you to the mouth of Labyrinth Canyon, which allows you the leisure of paddling the canyons and enjoying the day hikes without crossing the choppy, open channel. If you're underway by around 11 AM you'll arrive at the beach camp about noon. Set up camp and then slip into the gorgeous water and make your way into Labyrinth. With nearly a 360-degree view of formations such as Dominguez Butte, Gunsight Butte, Cookie Jar Butte, Alstrom Point, and Romana Mesa, the beauty of this area is impossible to put into words. Many a professional photographer has taken shots of these landmarks.

As you paddle through Labyrinth the canyon walls block the wind, and the water becomes glassy and smooth. At the end of the canyon you can pull the kayaks onto a muddy shore from which the water has only recently receded. Watch for quicksand—one of my friends hit a patch and sank up to his thighs. Needless to say, I wouldn't hike here alone. There are hanging gardens and seeps among the rocks that were underwater for decades before the recent drought. Even though the lake water has receded, the rocks sit under a hot desert sun and bleed water absorbed through the years.

Look out for tumbleweed as you hike up the slot canyon. They have a nasty set of thorns. Wear your shoes in the canyons and on the beaches.

Paddle back out and barbeque on the beach as the sun sets and the stars take their positions in the night sky.

DAY 2: Today, motor to a place near Face Canyon and park the boat in a side canyon (UTM 12 S 4771610/4096058). The shuttle guide stays with the group to take them to the mouth of each canyon. If you're going without a shuttle you'll need to factor in the extra paddling time.

Face Canyon is wider at first, and you'll pass several possible side canyon forays and beach camps. Some have lovely waterfalls and small canyon hikes. At the end of Face there is a nice slot canyon to explore. This is a full day's paddle, so set up camp in a spot that allows you to get out early the next day for the trip to West Canyon.

DAY 3: Head to West Canyon (UTM 12 S 4810662/4098979) for another full day of paddling. If you're heading back to the marina this evening, start the day's adventure early so you have plenty of time to do everything.

West Canyon is famous for its wonderful but challenging slot-canyon hiking—narrow caramel-colored walls, thin slots, wild gardens, an ankle-deep stream, and pools deep enough to swim through. The wet sand between your toes at times seems like a living thing, but if it jiggles it may be water-saturated quicksand, so watch out.

The waterfalls provide a unique challenge because you must find your way up them. The waterfalls and pools change from day to day depending on the water level in the small stream. West Canyon is more than 15 miles long, and when the water is running it can take a toll on hikers who are out of shape. Strength is important in many places. Just hike in as far as you like and then turn around and call it a day.

RESOURCES

TOURS AND GUIDES
Kayak Lake Powell: 1-888-854-7862; kyle@kayaklakepowell.com

USEFUL WEB SITES AND PHONE NUMBERS
Boat rentals, reservations, or marina information: 1-800-528-6154

Aramark Resort and Marina: www.lakepowell.com; the legal concessionaire for Lake Powell and owner of Wahweap and other marinas on the lake

Lake Powell Magazine: www.lakepowellmag.com; provides a collection of 24 maps that detail the canyons of Lake Powell

Carl Hayden and Glen Canyon Dam Visitors' Centers: 928-608-6404

National Park Service, Glen Canyon: www.nps.gov/glca; provides updated information such as marina closures and other current issues

Glen Canyon National History Association: www.glencanyonassociation.org

Wahweap Marina: 928-645-2433

National Park Service Medical Emergency: 1-800-582-4351; 24 hours a day

A LITTLE HISTORY, GEOLOGY, FLORA, AND FAUNA

Before Lake Powell filled the tributary canyons known collectively as Glen Canyon, this land was revered by people who visited regularly to experience the spirit of the towering orange walls, the twisting, rippled, reflective river, and the blue sky above.

There were canyons called Cathedral in the Desert, Mystery Canyon, and Music Temple. There were petroglyph panels and prehistoric artifacts like sandals, pots, pieces of woven cloth, and cliff dwellings with the thumbprints of ancient inhabitants still visible. People returned each year to run the river, hike among the hanging gardens, and listen to the songs and echoes of the canyons and chutes.

But in September of 1963 it all disappeared under Lake Powell, which is punctuated with the tops of these fabulous canyons—red cliff walls soaring hundreds of feet into the air, mesas, buttes, plateaus, all in a maze of 96 canyons and 186 miles of river channel. Since its beginning, the lake has been a place of political turmoil. The Glen Canyon Dam

Project was a result of the Colorado River Pact, which came about as the Bureau of Reclamation developed a water plan for the West.

The western states were divided into two groups, the Upper Basin states (Utah, Colorado, New Mexico, and Wyoming) and the Lower Basin states (Nevada, Arizona, and California). Each group was allotted a certain amount of water from the western waterways draining the Upper Basin states. A series of four dams were positioned to catch spring runoff and store it so the Lower Basin states would be able to receive their share during drier times. Congress passed this plan in 1956 and the Glen Canyon Dam Project began that same year.

Originally established for water allocation and distribution and hydroelectricity, the main function of the dam now seems to be tourism. In 1972 the region around Lake Powell was established as the Glen Canyon National Recreation Area, currently regulated by the National Park Service.

Glen Canyon has a vast and ancient history. Mammoth, bison, sloth, and camel dung have all been found in various canyons, dating their presence to nearly 13,000 years ago. Clay figurines and charcoal show human habitation in the area 8,900 years ago. Ancient Puebloans, Fremonts, Utes, and then Paiutes all spent time in the area, leaving pictographs, petroglyphs, cave dwellings, and other domestic remains as proof of a history now lost to the lake's waters. More recently, Spanish explorers, Mormon pioneers, and John Wesley Powell (for whom the lake is named) all left their mark on the area.

The canyons, buttes, and mesas in and around Lake Powell tell a geologic story of nearly 650 million years. Primarily sandstone, the stark cliffs provide a rich and colorful contrast to the blue waters of the lake. As the water level has dropped in recent years, more arches, Native American ruins, and petroglyph panels have become visible once again. One of the many intriguing aspects of the area lies in uncovering and rediscovery of things once lost.

Today, one nice thing about camping at Powell is the low insect population. Though there is plenty of water, the slickrock surrounding the lake doesn't provide the correct breeding environment for insect populations. In addition, lake waters start warming in June and usually maintain a comfortable temperature into October.

Lake Powell is home to Rainbow Bridge, the largest natural bridge on earth. It is one of the seven natural wonders of the world, and is considered a sacred site by Native Americans. Government agencies have worked with the Navajo, Hopi, Kaibab Paiute, San Juan Southern Paiute, and White Mesa Ute tribes to make sure that the area is managed in a culturally sensitive manner. It's possible to hike to this national monument.

Loading up the canoes

Canyonlands National Park

 STILLWATER CANYON

America's Best Western Flat Water

With world-class runs like Cataract Canyon, Westwater Canyon, and Lodore Canyon, Utah has plenty of big-water action for adrenaline junkies. But if you prefer to explore quietly on your own, then the Stillwater Canyon section of the Green River is the float for you. There is no big water, no crowds, but for the 2,500 to 3,500

153

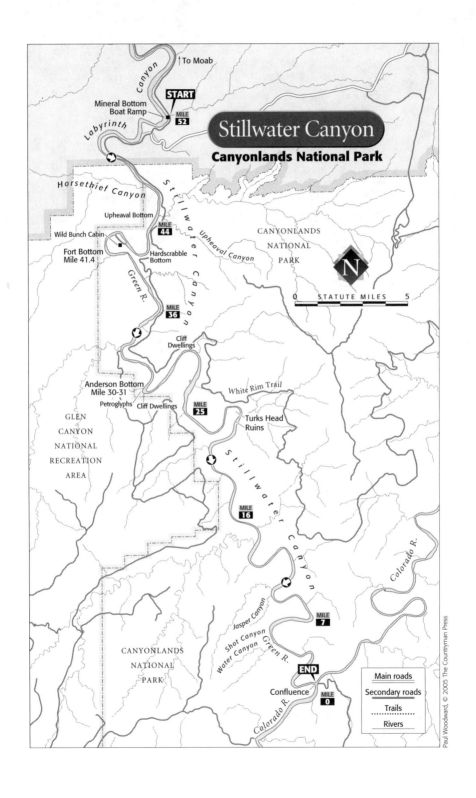

↑ To Moab

START
MILE **52**

Mineral Bottom
Boat Ramp

Canyon

Labyrinth

Stillwater Canyon
Canyonlands National Park

Horsethief Canyon

Stillwater

Upheaval Bottom

Upheaval Canyon

MILE **44**

Wild Bunch Cabin

Fort Bottom
Mile 41.4

Hardscrabble
Bottom

Canyon

Green R.

CANYONLANDS
NATIONAL
PARK

N

STATUTE MILES   5
0

MILE **36**

Cliff
Dwellings

Anderson Bottom
Mile 30-31

White Rim Trail

Petroglyphs   Cliff Dwellings

MILE **25**

Turks Head
Ruins

GLEN
CANYON
NATIONAL
RECREATION
AREA

Stillwater

MILE **16**

Canyon

Colorado R.

CANYONLANDS
NATIONAL
PARK

Jasper Canyon

Shot Canyon

Water Canyon

Green R.

MILE **7**

END

Confluence

MILE **0**

Colorado R.

Main roads

Secondary roads

Trails

Rivers

people a year that make the trip, the unrelenting canyon walls, the large number of pristine Native American pictographs and ruins, the incredibly varied hiking opportunities, and the comfortable sandbar campsites make a journey here a quasi-religious experience. This canyon is a temple to the best things the desert can be—pristine, isolated, beautiful, and deafeningly silent.

Stillwater Canyon is a four-day, 52-mile paddle from Mineral Bottom to the confluence of the Green and Colorado Rivers. No guides are allowed on this section of river, so all trips are self-guided adventures. Because continuing down the Colorado River from the confluence would put you into the whitewater of Cataract Canyon, and because it isn't feasible to paddle miles upstream to a take-out point, all trips through Stillwater Canyon require a jet-boat pickup at the confluence.

"This is where a name like Stillwater must come from," I wrote in my journal at 2 AM on my second night on the river. The moon was three-quarters full, lighting up the glassy mocha-colored water, the soaring uneven cliffs, and the sandy beach on which I had just walked. We were camped on a sandbar, the edge of which kept sloughing off into the river, reducing the beach chunk by sandy chunk. There was no wind. The world was moving yet absolutely still.

From the Island in the Sky Visitors' Center at Canyonlands National Park, you can see the Green River cutting a serpentine path through layer after layer of desert sandstone. Miles away, Stillwater Canyon appears just a few feet deep. Perspective is everything, though, and once you're in the canyon the river's smooth flow, the beauty and variety of the towering walls, and the stillness immerse you in another world.

Get ready for what many paddlers consider the West's best flat-water canoeing experience.

SPORT: Canoeing, camping

RATING: The paddling is easy on the meandering Class I flat water.

DISTANCE: Approximately 52 miles

Jaspar Canyon granary

TIME: Four or five days depending on river flow, wind, and your party's motivation. Plan on doing 3 or 4 miles per hour with a typical river flow in the 1,500–3,000 cfs range. You'll move slightly faster if you hit peak runoff between mid-May and mid-June, when flows are at 15,000–20,000 cfs. Use the flow rate to establish the number of miles you want to cover each day. On average, with a few stops, you'll be able to cover 15 to 20 miles per day in a canoe. But if wind becomes an issue, as it does on some afternoons, you may find yourself paddling hard to make your campsite before dark.

➡ GETTING THERE: From Salt Lake City, head south on I-15 toward Las Vegas. Merge left onto US 6 at Exit 261 near Spanish Fork about 50 miles south of Salt Lake. Head east on US 6 for approximately 125 miles to the junction with I-70 East. Follow I-70 for 23.2 miles to Exit 180, where you head south on US 191 toward Moab and Canyonlands National Park.

It's 20 miles to the junction with UT 313. Turn west up onto the Island in the Sky Mesa, from which you access Mineral Canyon. Halfway between mileposts 11 and 10, look for a sign for Horsethief Trail and Mineral Canyon Boat Ramp. Turn right on Horsethief Trail and travel 13 miles along uninspiring rolling desert to a set of dramatic steep switchbacks that descend into the canyon. At the bottom of the switchbacks, turn right and continue 0.67 mile to the Mineral Canyon Boat Ramp, the launch point for your trip.

Note: Because the only reasonable way out of the canyon at the end of the float is a jet-boat pickup by one of several Moab outfitters, your outfitter will likely drive you to the put-in at Mineral Bottom.

▶ RIVER: The Stillwater Canyon stretch covers approximately 52 miles of the last flat water on the Green River. From Mineral Bottom you paddle down to the confluence of the Green and Colorado Rivers, where you'll need to have a jet boat pick you up and take you 50 miles up the Colorado to the Potash Boat Ramp. Most outfitters in Moab will drive you to the put-in at the start of the trip and bring you back to town after the jet-boat ride.

MAXIMUM GROUP SIZE: Most groups range from four to six people, although parties as large as 40 are allowed.

▲ CAMPING: No designated campsites exist on the river, but you'll reduce your impact by camping on sandbars. Set up camp as close to the water as possible so high water will eventually erase any trace of your presence. Collect all food scraps to keep the ant and mouse populations in check.

The most popular month on the Stillwater section of the Green River is usually September, but any month between April and October may have high-use periods, and some boaters may have trouble finding an unoccupied campsite because of the lack of permit limitations. The National Park Service is currently working on a revision to the Canyonlands National Park river management plan, and is considering use limits for flat-water trips on the Green to reduce this problem.

There is one toilet at the Mineral Bottom launch site, but none on the river. Boaters must bring a washable, reusable toilet system that allows for the disposal of solid human waste, and all waste must be carried out. Toilet systems can be rented from area outfitters. All fires must be made in a fire pan. Burn the wood down to gray ash and then throw the ash in the river. If big chunks are left, please pack them out. Don't bury the ashes, as this has started fires in the past.

Be aware of possible flash floods when choosing a campsite. A small rainstorm a few miles away—and these are common in July and August—could inundate a poorly placed camp with a 4-foot wall of water in seconds. Also, as the river flow rises in May, be prepared for the possibility of a 2- to 3-foot increase in water level overnight. Mosquitoes may or may not give you trouble. They tend to be minimal after dry winters, but after heavy winters runoff can flood the riverbanks and spawn a massive mosquito population.

Based on these two constraints, your worst possible campsite would be the drainages at the immediate mouths of canyons, as they are possible death zones in a flash flood and tend to have standing water that is horribly infested with mosquitoes, even in good years.

Once mosquito season begins in late May, you'll find that sunny, dry, and windy places make the most pleasant campsites (i.e., sandbars). At high water in May and June most campsites will be "cowboy camps" on dry land, often under cottonwood trees above the river. With low water flows the rest of the year, you're likely to spend most nights on sandbars.

Wind is one of the biggest threats to paddlers. A strong wind can easily flip a canoe, so pull in close to shore if things get rough and make sure all your camps are as windproof as possible.

If you're planning to camp in the Moab area the night before your launch, Dead Horse Point State Park gives you a fabulous view of the Colorado River 2,000 feet below. The campground has 21 fully developed sites that can be reserved. Moab is full of additional camping

The jet-boat shuttle

options, with areas like Arches National Park just down the road and private campgrounds and national forests nearby.

SEASON: The prime months are March through October. The last week of March, all of April and most of May, and sometimes June are all busy times on the Green River. Spring and fall will be most pleasant, as the summers are exceedingly hot. Temperatures often run in excess of 100 degrees, but it is bearable if you spend a lot of time in the water.

Be aware that spring weather is unpredictable, with a significant amount of the year's precipitation falling in March and April. Violent afternoon thunderstorms arrive in July and August and they may force you to take cover at least once during a trip. High water in May and June can be intimidating for some boaters, and it cuts down on the number of available campsites. Early spring and mid- to late fall have brisk nights and pleasant days. If you're planning a lot of side hikes, these are ideal times of year.

Ⓟ **PERMITS:** Although required, permits are plentiful and more of a formality. The main constraint is reserving space with the outfitters for the car shuttle and jet-boat pickup. Arrange for permits with the Canyonlands National Park at 435-259-4351 or www.nps.gov/cany/reserve.htm.

The Park Service only allows two shuttle services to access the Green River. Tex's Riverways has been shuttling boats here since before Canyonlands was established, and Tag-a-Long Expeditions was later granted a license in the area in the name of capitalism and competition. The National Park Service tracks the number of users by permit, but at this time there are no restrictions on the number of permits they issue.

[$] **FEES:** A flat-water permit is $20; outfitter prices vary.

👕 **CLOTHING AND EQUIPMENT:** More and more Americans are visiting the Green River, and as Dirk Vaughn of Tex's Riverways says, "Most of mainstream America wants to do a river trip the way they do a backyard barbeque. They do not adapt themselves or their habits to the wilderness, they expect the wilderness to adapt to them."

Though canoes can hold a lot of stuff, you probably won't want to haul tons of gear up the riverbank to camp each night. Focus on the things that will be most important to you in a secluded area: first-aid kit, water, toilet, food, sunscreen, the appropriate clothes, and protection from insects. A set of binoculars will be helpful for catching sight of some of the ancient granaries.

Bring at least a gallon of water per person, per day, as hydration is very important here. A plastic cooler will keep food and drinks cold. Open it sparingly, and don't forget to bring duct tape to seal it each night. Block ice maintains its chill longer than crushed ice. Freezing water in milk jugs works well and ensures that you'll still have a cold drink available on day four. If your original supply of water runs out you can use river water. Obtain it from the center of the river channel, allow it to settle overnight, and then treat. Water can also be boiled for several minutes to make it potable.

Because the sun beats on you during the day and mosquitoes stick you in the evening, your best friends are going to be a wide-brimmed hat, a big bottle of waterproof sunscreen, and load of mosquito repellant. AfterBite liquid and cortisone cream can really help when you get bitten. You'll start out loving the sun and wanting to bare all, but after a couple of days it'll get old and you'll want to cover up. Bring a long-sleeved white shirt for comfort and protection. Also, for you international types, and for men very secure in their masculinity, you'll find a sarong to be extremely useful as a leg covering, a napkin/tablecloth, a bath towel, a sponge to clean your canoe, and even as a sail rigged between two paddles to make good time downwind.

Folding camp chairs are nice to have. A citronella candle works as both an excellent mosquito repellant and reading lamp. A tent with bug netting is a must. Since wood burning is not allowed without a fire pan, you'll need to bring a camp stove and fuel for cooking.

Dress for the season. Even in the summer you'll need a shell jacket and a fleece because it can get chilly if it rains and blows. Water-friendly sandals are a must. Be careful with fancy camera gear and sunglasses as the sand and grit in the water is murder on a lens.

Each group must bring a portable reusable toilet system to haul out all solid human waste. You will also need a toilet seat, toilet paper, hand soap, commercial holding-tank chemicals and deodorizers. Life jackets are optional through Stillwater Canyon, but mandatory on the Colorado from its confluence with the Green to Spanish Bottom.

SUGGESTED ITINERARY

Y ou'll need to cover a set amount of mileage each day to make it to the confluence in time to meet your jet boat, so plan accordingly.

At the Mineral Bottom Boat Ramp, check to make sure you have everything you need. Forgetting something here could be a real bummer, because once you're on the river you're committed. This ramp, at river mile 52.2 (with the confluence downstream being mile 0), is the beginning of your journey. At mile 49 you pass Point Bottom on the left and catch a glimpse of a road. This is part of the famous White Rim Trail (see chapter 9), which parallels your route for several miles. In one of the alcoves on river right, you might spot a small Ancestral Puebloan granary.

Between miles 45 and 46, or 6.75 miles from the launch point, Horsethief Canyon enters on the right. The tamarisk trees are thick here, but depending on the water level you may be able to paddle up the drainage for a hundred yards to a well-defined trail on the left. This area may be boggy at higher water, but at 5,000 cfs our party had no problem. It is only a short walk to a set of bighorn sheep petroglyphs and a hiking trail. This is part of the Horsethief Trail (UTM 12 S 0586201/4260302; elevation 3,944), which runs along river right from Moab. It's an old pioneer trail cow rustlers used to smuggle stolen cows out of the area (they crossed at Mineral Bottom). This is also the first obviously good campsite.

Back on the river, you're now in the most wide-open section of canyon on the trip. On river left at mile 43 is the entrance to Upheaval Canyon, site of Upheaval Dome. On a high point of the peninsula on river left 11.7 miles down from Mineral Bottom, at river mile 41.4, you'll find Fort Bottom (UTM 12 S 0584448/4256615; elevation 3,917), which has a Native American watchtower ruin.

The trail up to the ruin is easy to follow and starts at a sandbar on river left. Scramble up a short hill and go west on the well-worn trail out toward the point and up to the ruin. There is a scenic view of the river on both sides of the peninsula. You can scout for campsites or just take in the bird's eye perspective of the river. The ruin includes two cylindrical buildings and are made of flat stones stacked and mortared with mud. The hike up and back is relatively easy, and on the way you pass an old homesteader's cabin said to be visited by famous outlaws like Butch Cassidy and the Sundance Kid.

Around mile 36 White Rim sandstone rises out of the river at Potato Bottom. And at mile 32.5 you pass the mouth of Millard Canyon on your right. Flash floods have washed a lot of debris into the river here, creating a small set of riffles. Be careful and enjoy the thrill of this massive Class 1+ rapid! Looking up canyon to the southwest, you see the Butte of the Cross, named by John Wesley Powell, who mistakenly thought it was one single butte. But as you'll see later from Anderson Bottom, it's actually two separate buttes.

Between miles 30 and 31 you come to Anderson Bottom (UTM 12 S 0586126/4247152; elevation 3,934) on river right, which is definitely worth a stop. It's home to a petroglyph panel and a spring, handy if you're low on water. Exit river right. A footpath leads up and over to the right a hundred yards toward a natural amphitheater cut out of the cliff. The natural spring is in this amphitheater (UTM 12 S 0585945/4247330; elevation 3,852). A pipe has been inserted into a pool 30 feet up the wall, and when the water level is high enough, you can simply fill bottles from the pipe. An established footpath leads directly to the spring. Also nearby is an unused cave that the National Park Service dynamited into the wall to store items like toilets, signs, and other items.

To find the petroglyphs (UTM 12 S 0585801/4246880; elevation 3,957), walk on well-defined trails toward the rincon (a jutting hill) in the center of the bottom. The approach is sandy and steep in places, but the actual climb is only 100 or so vertical feet. It's 0.3 mile from the spring to the petroglyphs.

Look river left between miles 28 and 27 to see the remains of dwellings and granaries 100 feet up the cliff. At mile 27, halfway around Valentine Bottom on your right and 200 feet up the cliff, you can view a colorful pictograph panel and a cliff dwelling right at the joint between the white and red layers. You can see it plainly with binoculars, but a hike through the tamarisks brings you within 100 vertical feet, where the detail is much more impressive.

A small unnamed canyon appears on the right at mile 24.5. There is a nice dwelling on the right side of the canyon wall, 75 feet up in an alcove facing due east. And just to the left of the canyon entrance is a great two-story dwelling.

Around Turk's Head at mile 20.5, just where the cliff meets the river on the right, there is a great place to tie up for a hike to some granaries. Follow the base of the cliff to the north about 2,000 feet and look up 20 feet in an alcove to see a pair of them. With a bit of scrambling, you can actually get up to see the detail in the construction. Keep moving along the base of the cliff to see a third granary.

The canyon starts to close in around mile 19, and it remains narrower down to the confluence. There's not much in the way of ruins in the next 10 river miles, but the scenery is some of the best on the journey.

At mile 9, Jasper Canyon enters from the right (UTM 12 S 0594579/4233531; elevation 3,878). There are some great camp-sites here, as well as a nice granary along the base of the cliffs to the right. The granary is on the left side of the drainage as you're looking up at the big Jasper dry fall. The marks of fingers press-ing mortar into place are still visible, and there is a striking rock design above the doorway that seems to have a pattern.

Jasper Canyon is the only canyon on this side of the river in Canyonlands National Park that was never grazed, so it has been set aside for ecological study, which is fine because the climb into the canyon is extremely sketchy and exposed anyway.

The entrance to Shot and Water Canyons comes in on the right at mile 4.5. These canyons are absolutely gorgeous and actu-ally offer the best one-day access to the Maze area of Canyonlands from the river. You can't take out right at the mouth of the canyon because the tamarisk are too thick, but it's possible to pull over upriver of the canyon at one of the rocky outcroppings and make your way across. Water and Shot have the same entry point, but then split. A beautiful trail starts on the right side of the entrance to the canyon and goes all the way up Water Canyon. There's often a nice waterfall there.

Shot Canyon veers off just before the waterfall. Follow cairns or improvise. From the top of Water Canyon, you can see the chocolate spire of Chimney Rock a half mile to the west.

Back in the canoes, paddle down to the confluence, find a nice sandbar, and wash out your canoe while you wait for the jet boat to arrive. The confluence of the Green and Colorado Rivers marks the coming together of two of the Southwest's great waterways; the Colorado River a gigantic force from this point on.

The jet boat takes you up the Colorado 50 miles (two or three hours) to the Potash Boat Ramp, 20 miles from Moab down Potash Road/UT 279.

IN CASE OF EMERGENCY: You can exit the river at places along the White Rim Trail down to river mile 33, after which access is no longer available. Below that point your only option is to check with other groups on the river to see if they have medical knowledge or if they can contact a park ranger or patrol at the end of their trip. Another option would be to signal any passing aircraft with a small mirror.

RESOURCES

SHUTTLES AND RENTALS
Tex's Riverways: 435-259-5101; www.texsriverways.com
Tag-a-Long Expeditions: 1-800-453-3292; www.tagalong.com

USEFUL WEB SITES AND PHONE NUMBERS
Dead Horse Point State Park: 1-800-322-3770 or 435-259-2614 (reservations); www.state.ut.us/parks/www1dead.htm
Arches National Park: 435-259-8161
National Park Service, Canyonlands: www.nps.gov/cany
USGS Stream Flow data site: http://nwis.waterdata.usgs.gov/nwis

A LITTLE HISTORY, GEOLOGY, FLORA, AND FAUNA

A s you move down this last 52 miles of the Green River, you are literally slicing through time, through the millions of years of sediment that formed Canyonlands. Beginning at Mineral Bottom you'll notice the sheer cliffs of Navajo sandstone sitting on a layer of crumbly Kayenta, sitting on top of another sheer vertical layer of Wingate sandstone. Below the Wingate is a broken layer called the Chinle Formation (which is where uranium is found), and at river level the Gaudi-like rusted red of the Moenkopi Formation appears.

Downriver at mile 38, the solid, capped, White Rim appears. Around mile 32, Organ Rock shale shows up beneath the White Rim, and the Cutler Formation is visible at mile 28. As you round Turk's Head, at mile 21, Cedar Mesa sandstone—the main component of the Maze area of Canyonlands—rises out of the river. Around mile 12 begin looking for the Lower Cutler Formation. By the time you reach the confluence, the Upper Hermosa layer will have appeared.

Tamarisk trees are the most obvious plant life you'll see. They form a veritable forest along the riverbanks. Introduced to the Southwest as early as the 1700s, and used by local ranchers to prevent erosion and as windbreaks, tamarisk trees have been so successful here that they've gradually taken over and pushed out native species. You'll also see a fair amount of prickly-pear cactus. Archaeologists believe the large strands of prickly pear that dot the banks of the Green River today are the remnant of Ancestral Puebloan prickly-pear farms. Once the needles are removed, the lobes can be cooked, as any veteran traveler to Mexico knows. The fruit, which ripens in July, is something like a kiwi crossed with a raspberry.

Opportunities for wildlife viewing are plentiful. You'll likely see great blue herons, ravens, Colorado chipmunks, kit foxes, desert bighorn sheep, and the faded rattlesnake. There are many animals in the desert, but they often go unseen because most are nocturnal. Animals stay cool and conserve energy and moisture by resting during the heat of the day. You might spot mountain sheep traversing the desert cliffs, and you're likely to catch a glimpse of a beaver if you drift close to the riverbank without making a sound.

A surprising number and variety of peoples have lived along these river bottoms. The Archaic Culture lived here 8,000 to 9,000 years ago. The most sophisticated rock art is generally attributed to the Archaic People. The Ancestral Puebloans were here 700 to 1,000 years ago. Their granaries for food storage are still found in dozens of high, inaccessible places along the river, evidently built there to protect food from scavengers. A close examination shows waddle-and-daub-like construction, with stones piled up and sealed with bits of leaves, mud, and sticks—a formula that has lasted for hundreds of years.

While John Wesley Powell was the most famous early western explorer to come downriver, a French trapper named Denis Julien came through as early as 1836. More recently, around the turn of the century, cattlemen and farmers variously settled in the river bottoms. The remote canyons once harbored cattle rustlers, and in the 1920s they gave refuge to dozens of entrepreneurial moonshiners.

Mexican Hat Rock

San Juan River

A Watery Path into History

Running the San Juan River is not just about water. It's about the blistering desert sun, and nights under brilliant stars; it's about the bite of ants, the great blue heron, the herd of bighorn sheep; it's about layers of fine red silt coating everything from each strand of hair to the floor of your tent; its about pioneer trails, failed prospecting, and colorful thousand-foot cliff walls that display the strata of eons and Native American petroglyphs and dwelling sites; it's about a reprieve

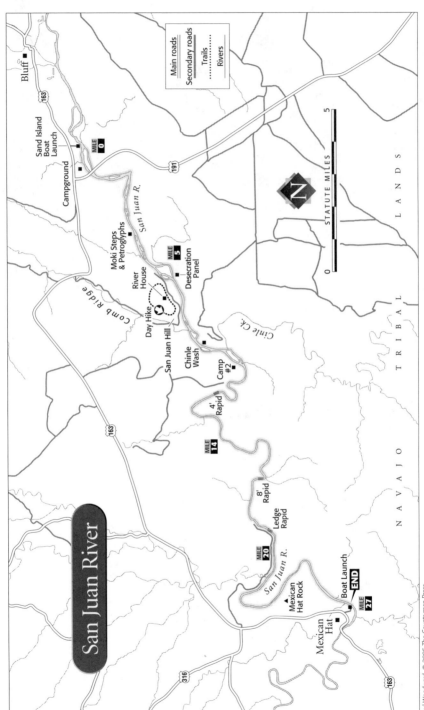

San Juan River

Bluff

163

Sand Island
Boat Launch

Campground

MILE 0

San Juan R.

Moki Steps
& Petroglyphs

MILE 5

River
House

Desecration
Panel

Comb Ridge

Day Hike

191

San Juan Hill

Chinle
Wash

Camp
#2

Cinle Ck.

4'
Rapid

MILE 14

163

8'
Rapid

Ledge
Rapid

MILE 20

San Juan R.

Mexican
Hat Rock

Boat Launch

END

MILE 27

Mexican
Hat

316

163

TRIBAL   LANDS

NAVAJO

Main roads
Secondary roads
Trails
Rivers

N

STATUTE MILES

0   5

Paul Woodward, © 2005 The Countryman Press

from everyday life, sharing time with friends, and of course the prehistoric river feeding an arid desert.

The San Juan River flows through the southeastern corner of Utah. Although it's a relatively easy river to negotiate, you still need to know what you're doing and have the proper equipment. It's a fast river—faster than it looks—with a rate of drop (on average) that is equal to the Colorado River's through the Grand Canyon.

This three-day trip combines pleasant time on the river with side excursions that explore geology, history, and ancient civilization. You'll pass Navajo sandstone and canyon walls streaked with desert varnish, and you'll see petroglyph sites every day, along with ancient hand and footholds at the Moki Steps area.

Over 13,000 boaters float the San Juan each year, only slightly less than the number in the Grand Canyon. The area is strictly regulated to keep the environment clean and enjoyable for everyone. The few rapids on the San Juan are mellow and cooling, making it a river for all ages and abilities. If you aren't an experienced rafter, go with a river-rafting company that will take care of your group and also guide you through the side trips and the area's geology and history.

The most popular launch site is Sand Island near the town of Bluff, an extremely small town with little to offer beyond the bed & breakfasts, lodges, and motels in which river-runners stay. The town is also home to Wild Rivers Expeditions, the only guiding operation in the immediate area. There is a gas station/drug store and a couple of small restaurants, all of which seem to rely on the river's tourist industry.

SPORT: River rafting, hiking, sight-seeing

RATING: Easy; Class II and III rapids

DISTANCE: 27.5 river miles, from Sand Island to Mexican Hat

TIME: Three days

GETTING THERE: To reach Bluff from Salt Lake City, head south on I-15 to Spanish Fork, and then turn east on US 6. Follow US 6 until it turns

Floating the San Juan

into US 191, which takes you past Moab and on to Bluff. It's a 6.5-hour drive from Salt Lake City to Bluff.

RIVER: A soft meandering river, the San Juan has few rapids (none above Class III). The river is one of the siltiest in the world. It starts out as a clear mountain stream in the San Juan Mountains of Colorado, but by the time it reaches Lake Powell it's carrying 30 to 40 percent of the sediment that settles into the lake. This sediment causes the sand waves that seem to shift and disappear before your eyes. It's a big muddy river, just like a desert waterway should be.

Water levels in the river are predominantly determined by releases from Navajo Dam in northern New Mexico. I ran the chocolate waters of the San Juan when it was running at 3,000 cubic feet per second (cfs), which was higher than it had been all season. The ride was pleasant and there weren't a great many sandbars to navigate around. River flow is highest during May and June. In September 2003, flow peaked at a whopping 20,000 cfs, so always monitor the water level before your trip.

If three days on the water just aren't enough, you can spend a full week floating the San Juan. Put in at Sand Island and take out at Clay Hill Crossing—an 83-mile trek. The extra time on the water is well worth the effort because the lower half of the river has more Class II and III rapids and less people.

MAXIMUM GROUP SIZE: No more than 25 people.

CAMPING: All campsites are assigned when you pick up your permit. They are nothing more than sandy beaches that you must leave looking better than you found them. All structures erected during your stay at camp should be deconstructed before you launch the next day.

River-use regulations require that all groups bring a washable, leak-proof, reusable toilet system that allows solid human body waste to be carried out for disposal. Most rafters use the "groover," a military system consisting of an ammo can and toilet seat. The name comes from the marks it leaves if you forget the seat. It has a tight lid that can be locked during travel on the river. Fire pans are required, and all ash must be removed. Both items can be acquired at river supply web sites such as www.pacificriversupply.com.

SEASON: May and June are the most popular months for running the San Juan. This is also when water levels are at their highest. If you're unable to get a permit for the May/June time slot, take heart; it's easier to secure a spot from July through October.

PERMITS: Permits are required year-round. They are only issued through advance reservation to individuals at least 18 years old. A launch reservation may be obtained through a pre-season drawing or a post-drawing telephone reservation. The BLM office must have your permit application on file to process a launch reservation request. To participate in the pre-season drawing your application must be received prior to

February 1. There is no need to submit fees until after you obtain a reservation. Permits are issued through the BLM San Juan Field Office, P.O. Box 7, Monticello, Utah 84535; 435-587-1544.

If you don't receive a launch date you can check online for available dates at www.blm.gov/utah/monticello/river.htm. The dates shown in red are unavailable. These change daily due to cancellations and new permits being issued. You may apply for up to three launch dates on your application card, but only one launch per group will be awarded through drawing. If you don't hear anything by March 1, you didn't draw a launch. You may call the BLM office regarding the availability of launches on the first business day after that date.

The easiest way to guarantee a launch date is to go with a rafting company. On a guided trip, the company secures all permits and provides guides, food, and all waste removal. Some tour companies, like Wild Rivers, provide guides with expertise in the geology and history of the San Juan and its inhabitants, but many don't. Be sure to confirm that the outfitter provides side trips and knowledgeable guides when you book your trip.

$ FEES: The current permit fee for a trip from Sand Island to Mexican Hat is $6 per person. The seven-day trip from Sand Island to Clay Hills is $18 per person. Contact the BLM at www.blm.gov/utah/monticello/river.htm to check for up-to-date fees.

River outfitter fees run $525 to $1,200 depending on the length of the trip. They typically provide everything but your clothing, tent, sleeping bag, and personal items. Travelers provide their own alcoholic beverages, if desired.

CLOTHING AND EQUIPMENT: You are required to pack lightly because of limited space, and everything will need to be loaded into a dry bag. Essential items include a lightweight, compact sleeping bag and pad, sunscreen, good sunglasses with a tie-on strap, and a personal water bottle. Lip balm with sunblock, a long-sleeved white shirt, and long pants will protect you from the desert sun. It only takes one day to get too much sun, and then you just want protection. I spent days with a wet towel over my legs to keep my body temperature down and my legs out

River House

of the sun. A good hat with a wide brim and a bandana you can wet and place over your head will also keep you cool.

A sturdy pair of water sandals is very important, particularly when getting in and out of the boat while the muddy bottom sucks at your feet. My sandals lasted until the last day of the trip and then were retired to a bail bucket at the front of the raft. Never leave the insect repellant behind on a river trip, although the bugs here aren't usually too bad. Good lotion, aloe products, and wet wipes will keep your skin clean and hydrated. Another item I found indispensable on the river was my compact travel chair. It's wonderful to eat or relax on the beach in comfort. Don't forget a headlamp, waterproof camera, hiking shoes, light jacket, towel, and the obvious toiletries such as toothbrush and deodorant. Last but not least, don't forget to throw in your tent.

Most people on our river trip wore shorts and long-sleeved shirts each day. T-shirts and tank tops are great, but plan to wear a lot of sunscreen. Wrap-around sarongs are popular on these trips, and we only needed our rain jackets one time during the voyage. Don't wear anything you can't replace, as the red river silt digs deep into everything; you may not be able to get your clothing clean after the trip.

This trip is family friendly because of the easy flow of water, but make sure to protect your children from the sun and the heat. Drink a lot of water and sport drinks to keep yourself hydrated. The San Juan is too silty for filtering, so you'll have to bring enough water for the entire trip. If you're on a guided tour the outfitter will take care of all your non-alcoholic drinking needs. Sunstroke and heat exhaustion can sneak up on you here if you don't drink more than you think you need.

The riverbanks often have thorns from Russian olive trees, sharp beaver-chewed sticks, the occasional scorpion, and ubiquitous sticker weeds, so I recommend wearing shoes at all times. Some people on our trip wore socks with their sandals, but the socks attracted more weeds and stickers than bare legs.

For unguided trips, the BLM requires that you have the following: (1) a first-aid kit adequate for the size of your group; (2) a repair kit with adequate materials to repair the types of boats you are using; (3) an air pump to inflate boats after repairs; (4) a washable, leak-proof reusable toilet system; (5) a durable metal fire pan, at least 12 inches wide with at least a 1.5-inch lip around its outer edge and sufficient to contain fire and remains; (6) a properly sized white-water type I, II, III, or V life jacket for each member of your group.

Also, each raft, dory, or canoe must have an extra oar, paddle, or motor capable of maneuvering the vessel, a bail bucket or bilge pump, and a rescue rope. Each trip leader is responsible for ensuring that all trip participants carry out all charcoal, fire ash, garbage, and solid human body wastes. You'll need dry bags to store your clothes and personal items, as well as coolers and large water containers for all your potable water and perishables.

SUGGESTED ITINERARY

Make sure to send your launch reservation application to the BLM prior to February 1 for the year you plan to float, or contact a river outfitter to book your trip.

Arrive in Bluff the day before you plan to launch so you can get an early start the next day. Just loading the boats is a lengthy process. The launch site at Sand Island is actually a BLM campground with picnic tables and non-potable water. There are a couple of motels and bed & breakfasts and a lodge in Bluff if you don't want to camp. The campsites noted here are the ones I used on my trip down the San Juan, but keep in mind that all campsites are assigned when your permit is issued.

DAY 1: Depart from the Sand Island launch ramp 4 miles west of Bluff. As the float begins, the river meanders through Navajo sandstone marked with bold black streaks of desert varnish. This area is called Tiger Wall. At river mile 3.5 (UTM 12 S 0619710/4122353), pull the raft to river right and take a short walk to a site called the Moki Steps. These wall divots are hand and footholds that were carved into the rock by ancient inhabitants of the area. After finding the steps, head west along the wall to view ancient petroglyphs dating back 2,000 years (UTM 12 S 0619788/4122524). If you look closely you may find shards of scattered pottery in the sand.

At river mile 4 (UTM 12 S 0618487/4121979), directly west of the landing site, there's a big cottonwood tree at Butler Wash that provides a peaceful, shady respite for lunch. Look up at the wall behind the tree to the southwest for another panel of petroglyphs. Approximately 400 yards downriver is the Lower Butler Wash Panel, a petroglyph site sacred to both ancient and modern Native Americans.

Shortly after mile 5 on river left you come to a spot where you can land and hike to a petroglyph site named Desecration Panel

(UTM12 S 0617728/4120511). The story is that a local Navajo family experiencing a terrible misfortune defaced this wall of petroglyphs in the 1950s. The Navajo believe witchcraft can be tied to images, and the ritual response within the Indian culture was to deface and "rub out" many of the images on this wall. The Navajo Reservation runs along the south bank of the San Juan.

Desecration Panel is one of the only rock art sites on river left. From the landing, follow a wide trail up the hill. Head left at the top and go farther down the wall to locate the desecrated images, which appear to have been carefully chosen, as only certain ones were bludgeoned.

A great camping beach sits at mile 5 just in front of River House, one of the best preserved ruins on the river. Your campsite will depend on the assignment you were given when you got your permit, but shoot for this area if possible. On our first night we learned to anchor our tents with rocks instead of just tent stakes because the wind pulled the stakes out of the sand.

DAY 2: This day is spent primarily on land, with only 3 miles of float time. Start by exploring River House, a Pueblo III site dating to A.D. 1250 (UTM 12 S 0616398/4120385). To get there from the campsite, head northeast to the rear of the camp and follow a sandy trail to the right. River House is 0.31 mile up the trail, about an 8-minute walk.

The sections of the structure protected by the natural alcove in which it was built are still well preserved. You can easily decipher the kiva (a round ceremonial structure) and multiple storage and living rooms. There are a few petroglyphs on the cliff above the dwelling, including a giant snake weaving its way across the wall. You'll spot more snakes creeping along the wall to the west. To see remnants of granaries, stay on the upper path and head west. They are built into the cliff walls.

Be careful not to lean or climb on the walls, as they are fragile. Show respect when visiting sites like River House and leave all pot shards and other items like arrowheads where you find them.

Follow the trail/road up and around to San Juan Hill, which leads to Comb Ridge, a Mormon wagon trail leading over a rugged 700-foot-high cliff wall. The ridge offers a magnificent view of the river ahead and is worth the climb (UTM 12 S 0615554/4120867; elevation 4,671).

When the Mormon pioneers attempted to settle the region, the ridge was such an obstacle that an ox supposedly died in the yoke as it struggled against the grade. The unpredictability of water levels in the San Juan River destroyed all the pioneer's attempts at irrigation and farming, forcing the settlement to pull back to Blanding, where farming was less brutal. You'll also see remnants of an old mill and Barton's Trading Post in this area.

Back on the river, a 2-mile float to Chinle Wash brings you to painted rock art and cliff dwellings hidden among rock alcoves. Chinle Wash is located just before mile 8 on river left. Land the rafts and hike south/southeast until you pick up a trail that winds back about a mile into granaries and the remains of cliff dwellings. I sat at the base of the granaries while the rest of my party moved on ahead to the caves that held remnant desert brick. In the silence I could picture the ancient inhabitants climbing the walls to reach their stores of food. I listened to the hum of insect life in the hot, dry air and laid quietly in the shade on a flat rock, feeling the heartbeat of the desert.

One mile downriver we set up camp for the night. From here, the majority of the sandstone disappears and the Honaker Trail Formation begins.

DAY 3: This is the longest water day. From river mile 9 to the take-out point near mile 29, there's no need to stop for anything but lunch. Today you go through Four-Foot Rapid near mile 11.5 and Eight-Foot Rapid at mile 17. At mile 19 you hit Ledge Rapid and around mile 23 you can see Mexican Hat Rock, a balancing rock off to the right that looks like an upside down sombrero.

The boat ramp is easy to spot on river right. The road from the ramp at Mexican Hat connects with UT 163, which takes you back to Bluff.

RESOURCES

TOURS AND GUIDES

Wild Rivers Expeditions: 1-800-422-7654; www.riversandruins.com
BLM River Office: 435-587-1544; www.blm.gov/utah/monticello/river.htm

USEFUL WEB SITES AND PHONE NUMBERS

Sand Island Campground: 435-587-1500; fee charged
Desert Rose Inn and Cabins: 1-888-475-ROSE; www.desertroseinn.com;
    $50–$75
Pioneer House Bed & Breakfast: 1-888-637-2582; www.pioneerhouseinn.com;
    $50–$100+
Bureau of Reclamation (to check water levels/dam releases): 970-385-6560

A LITTLE HISTORY, GEOLOGY, FLORA, AND FAUNA

The San Juan River has a 12,000-year history of human occupation. Though the lower San Juan in Utah wasn't as widely occupied as the upper San Juan in Colorado, it served as an overflow for various Native American tribes. Rock art in the area has dated the civilizations of the San Juan to as far back as 4000 B.C. The incredible amount of artifacts in the area were largely undisturbed until the 19th century, dry desert heat preserving remnants of civilizations from 700 to 8,000 years ago.

The Southern Utes and San Juan Paiutes, both hunter-gatherer cultures, moved into the region between A.D. 1100 and 1500. Apache and Navajo tribes migrated into the Southwest around the same time, and the San Juan River served as a rough boundary for the various tribes. When Coronado came searching for gold in 1540 and Catholic missionaries came to tame the heathen, they found the tribes of the Southwest in a patchwork across the land. Between 1500 and 1600 almost 80 percent of the Native American population in the Southwest was destroyed by smallpox and measles brought by the Conquistadors.

In the mid-1800s, Mormon pioneers made their way west into the Great Salt Lake Valley and continued down into the southern reaches of what would become Utah. In 1879, the LDS church organized an expedition to establish a settlement in the San Juan area, which became known as the Hole-in-the-Rock expedition.

The 250 men, women, and children took 80 wagons and more than a thousand head of cattle and horses through some of the most difficult terrain in the country. They spent six long months blasting through rocks that barred the way, constructing a dug-way, and pulling their wagons up slopes so steep the exhausted horses repeatedly stumbled and bloodied the sandstone. When they finally settled Bluff, they struggled with the irregular surges of the river—flows as high as 70,000 cfs have been recorded—and ultimately were unable to maintain the irrigation ditches they needed to support farms and grazing lands. The group repeatedly asked church authorities for permission to leave the settlement, which was eventually granted.

The San Juan was host to a gold rush in 1892, and then an oil boom less than 10 years after the gold ran out. Both were short lived, but they brought prospectors and drillers to the area. The town of Mexican Hat was established when Emery Goodridge hit a 75-foot gusher. You can still spot a few small drills and oil rigs littering the landscape.

Today the river, like all western waterways, is part of a tug-of-war between Indian tribes, federal land agencies, farmers, and private and commercial river-runners. After the recreational boom in the 1930s, the San Juan became one of the premier river-running destinations in the country. In the 1960s, when the trend really started to take off, pristine areas of the southwestern waterways turned into smelly latrines and unsightly dumps. Land-management agencies were forced to step in and regulate river use.

Two major dams affect the river's ebb and flow: Navajo Dam in New Mexico upstream and Glen Canyon Dam downstream in Arizona, which stops the river's flow at Lake Powell. These dams have a major impact on the river, the surrounding communities, and the ecosystems that depend on the flow of water. They're a primary source of water for some of the most arid land in the United States and regulate most of the extreme flooding while submerging the last 70 miles of the river. Controversy over their effects on the landscape of the Southwest led to the emergence of the environmental movement.

Two types of trees line the banks of the San Juan: the tamarisk, a non-native tree from the Middle East that consumes 200 gallons of water a day, and the Russian olive, an exotic species introduced into the West for erosion control. The tamarisk, or salt cedar, has drooping braches and pink plumes with showy flowers. It uses such incredible amounts of water and chokes the riverbanks with so much undergrowth that it's now a very unwelcome presence in the West. The Russian olive has silver-gray leaves and prominent thorns that are hard as nails and can go right through the sole of a sandal. Still, during spring months it fills the air with a divine scent that always makes me close my eyes and breathe deeply.

Desert wildlife here is variegated but secretive. A herd of bighorn sheep lives along the banks of the San Juan between Comb Ridge and Lime Creek. With exception of one old ram, the entire herd uses the south side of the river on the land of the Navajo Nation. If you watch carefully you may catch a glimpse of one or more.

A friend of mine once set his sweatshirt down while hiking and returned to find a good-sized scorpion nestled in its folds. And if you aren't careful with food scraps, hordes of ants will descend upon your camp and literally drive you off with their burning bites. You'll see beaver dams as you float downriver, and you may even catch a glimpse of a swimming beaver. Coyotes are heard more than they're seen, but great blue herons are a daily sight. There are also ravens and cliff swallows, lizards and squirrels. With enough time on the river, you'll have a good chance to see them all.

Nine native fish species once swam in the San Juan, but with the introduction of catfish and carp for sport fishing, dams that interfere with migratory patterns, and the pollution from oil operations, the Colorado pikeminnow and razorback sucker are now on the endangered species list. It's already too late for some species, but federal agencies are spending millions of dollars to protect and restore the native fish community that still exists.

The Green River

Green River

DESOLATION AND GRAY CANYONS

Solitude and Simplicity in Utah's Deepest Canyon

John Wesley Powell, on his historic and heroic 1869 expedition down
the Green River through what would later become Utah's Green
River Wilderness, described Desolation Canyon this way:

*Crags and tower-shaped peaks are seen everywhere, and above
them long lines of broken cliffs; beyond the cliffs are pine forests of
which we obtain occasional glimpses as we look up through a vista
of rocks. We are minded to call this the Canyon of Desolation.*

183

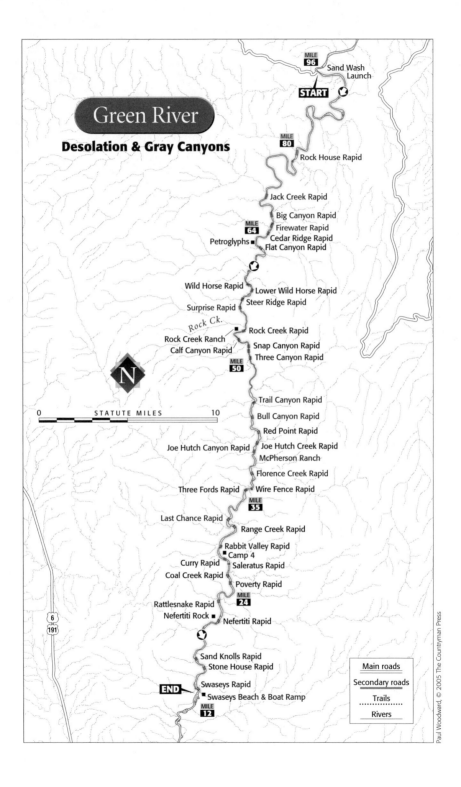

Green River

Desolation & Gray Canyons

MILE 96 — Sand Wash Launch
START

MILE 80 — Rock House Rapid

Jack Creek Rapid

Big Canyon Rapid
Firewater Rapid
MILE 64 — Cedar Ridge Rapid
Petroglyphs — Flat Canyon Rapid

Wild Horse Rapid — Lower Wild Horse Rapid
Surprise Rapid — Steer Ridge Rapid

Rock Ck.

Rock Creek Rapid
Rock Creek Ranch — Snap Canyon Rapid
Calf Canyon Rapid — Three Canyon Rapid
MILE 50

N

0 — STATUTE MILES — 10

Trail Canyon Rapid

Bull Canyon Rapid

Red Point Rapid

Joe Hutch Canyon Rapid — Joe Hutch Creek Rapid
McPherson Ranch

Florence Creek Rapid

Three Fords Rapid — Wire Fence Rapid
MILE 35

Last Chance Rapid

Range Creek Rapid

Rabbit Valley Rapid
Camp 4
Curry Rapid — Saleratus Rapid
Coal Creek Rapid

Poverty Rapid
MILE 24

Rattlesnake Rapid
Nefertiti Rock — Nefertiti Rapid

Sand Knolls Rapid
Stone House Rapid

END — Swaseys Rapid
Swaseys Beach & Boat Ramp
MILE 12

6 / 191

| Main roads |
| Secondary roads |
| Trails |
| Rivers |

Paul Woodward, © 2005 The Countryman Press

Located in east-central Utah, Desolation and Gray Canyons are so far removed from civilization that outfitters actually fly most of their clients to the launch site. The same aspects of the river that left Powell and his crew with such a feeling of desolation now attract river-runners from around the world. This family-friendly adventure through Utah's deepest canyon boasts nearly 50 easy to moderate rapids, with sandy beaches, historic ranches, outlaw hideouts, petroglyphs, hoodoos, and towering cottonwood trees along the way.

SPORT: River rafting

RATING: Easy to moderate, with Class I, II, and III rapids

DISTANCE: 84 river miles

TIME: Three days with a motor; five or six days if paddling

GETTING THERE: If you use one of the Moab outfitters for this trip you will most likely arrive at the Sand Wash launch site by airplane. And they'll make arrangements to get you back to Moab from the take-out at Swaseys Beach. If your party goes unguided, you'll leave a vehicle at the Swaseys Beach ramp, and then shuttle the raft, rafters, and equipment to the launch at Sand Wash. Note also that rafters can take a flight to Sand Wash and meet the driver there.

From Salt Lake City, travel south on I-15 to Exit 261, where you merge east onto US 6. After 152 miles, join US 191 via Exit 180 toward Moab on the way to the I-70 junction. Head east for a few miles on I-70, and then take US 191 south to Moab. The airport is 18 miles north of town; you pass it on the way in. Parking is free.

The air-taxi services at the Moab airport and Green River airstrip are familiar with the flight to the Desolation Canyon launch site. It's 80.3 nautical miles from the Moab airport to Sand Wash, with a flight time of 46 minutes. If you're leaving from the town of Green River, it's 53 nautical miles and 30 minutes.

Sand Wash Launch Site. If you're driving to the Sand Wash launch site, follow the above directions toward Moab, but when you get to

View of airstrip near Sand Wash launch site

Wellington on US 6/191 take a left at Soldier Creek Road, which is right next to the only Chevron station in town. This road is paved for 12.5 miles and then changes to well-packed dirt. At 21.8 miles you enter Nine Mile Canyon, home to an array of petroglyph panels, old ranching cabins, and cowboy hangouts.

Thirty-eight miles from where you turned onto Soldier Creek, turn left on a signed road toward the Sand Wash/Green River access. Five miles farther on, turn right at a sign for Sand Wash. Stay on the main road for an additional 25.2 miles, being careful to avoid taking any of the spur roads. The road is signed at appropriate junctions. The last couple of miles take you down a gravel wash to the launch site and a ranger station. It's possible to access the launch site with a two-wheel-drive vehicle. It's roughly a three-hour drive from the turnoff at Wellington, covering 68.2 miles.

Swaseys Beach Take-out. To drive your shuttle vehicle and trailer to the take-out at Swaseys Beach, go a few minutes north on Hastings Road in the town of Green River. Swaseys is an hour from Moab. Drive time one way from Sand Wash to Swaseys Beach via Nine Mile Canyon for the shuttle is 4.5 to 5 hours, assuming good roads and weather conditions. Three of those hours are on dirt roads.

RIVER: The majority of the Green River is calm, with slight riffles and Class I, II, and III rapids. The rapids increase in difficulty as you travel downriver. Steer Ridge Rapid lies hidden around a bend and has tossed many an unsuspecting boater. In the 83-mile float through Desolation Canyon and into Gray Canyon, the water is full of silt (as most desert rivers are), but a clear fresh spring enters eventually.

MAXIMUM GROUP SIZE: Groups are limited to 25.

CAMPING: Selecting campsites on the river is simply a matter of finding a nice sandy beach, preferably with a big cottonwood tree to provide shade. All boaters are required to carry their own toilet systems in and out. These must be leakproof and follow certain requirements. The BLM will explain these when you get your permit. If you go with a river guide, all those little details will be taken care of.

SEASON: Water levels in the river are controlled by snowfall and dam releases. The water is higher during spring, but warmer and better for swimming in July and August. For information on water levels call 801-539-1311 or visit www.cbrfc.gov. Flows as low as 900 cfs are adequate for most boaters.

PERMITS: All parties must have a BLM permit. If you go with a commercial outfitter, they'll take care of securing permits. Three guided and three private launches are allowed daily. There is a pre-season drawing for launches from April 1 through October 31. To participate, your application must be received prior to February 1. The lottery for permits is held on this day, and you will be contacted with a letter by the end of February if you drew a launch permit.

If your private party didn't get a permit, you can make a post-drawing telephone reservation starting on the first business day of March. Contact the BLM Price Field Office at 435-636-3622 or www.blm.gov/utah/price/riverinf.htm.

$ FEES: For private parties, the fee is $18 per person. Costs for commercial guides run around $500 to $800.

CLOTHING AND EQUIPMENT: Bringing the right equipment is crucial on a river trip that takes you into country this far removed from modern life. For a successful white-water adventure, bring only the things you really need; extra items will become cumbersome. Everything you take needs to fit in a dry bag, with your sleeping bag, foam pad, and tent or ground cloth topping the list. All toiletries and clothes must fit as well. Dry bags are generally the size of a medium backpack, although they're available in a variety of dimensions.

Sun is a huge factor on the river. Make sure you bring a good hat with a wide brim, sunscreen, lip balm with sunblock, and good sunglasses with a leash. A long-sleeved white shirt and long pants will also help protect you. It takes only a few hours to get too much sun. Wet towels spread across your legs or shoulders will help keep you cool, as will a wet bandana placed over the head.

Hydration is critical. Bring in all potable water. On day three you'll come to a freshwater spring from which you can pull water, but it still needs to be filtered. Sport drinks that help replace lost electrolytes make a big difference, too. Perishable food and large water containers can be kept in coolers with block ice.

Other essential items, in no particular order, include a sturdy pair of water sandals, insect repellant, good lotion and aloe products, wet wipes, compact travel chair, headlamp, waterproof camera, hiking shoes, light

Stopping for lunch

jacket, towel, and a swimsuit or water clothing. Wrap-around sarongs are a staple on the river. If you're making this a family trip, remember the squirt guns, sand pails, and other fun toys.

If you're organizing your own trip, the BLM requires that you provide the following: (1) a first-aid kit matched to the size of your group; (2) a repair kit with adequate materials to repair the types of boat you are using; (3) an air pump to inflate boats after repairs; (4) a washable, leakproof reusable toilet system that allows for the carry-out and disposal of solid human body waste; (5) a durable metal fire pan, at least 12 inches wide with at least a 1.5-inch lip around its outer edge and sufficient to contain fire and remains; (6) and a properly sized white-water type I, II, III, or V life jacket for each member of your group.

Each raft, dory, or canoe must have an extra oar, paddle, or motor capable of maneuvering the vessel, a bail bucket or bilge pump, and a rescue rope. Each trip leader is responsible for ensuring that participants carry all charcoal, fire ash, garbage, and solid human body wastes out of the river area. When securing your permit, check the regulations for any updates.

SUGGESTED ITINERARY

DAY 1: If you're flying, the chartered air taxi will take you to a mesa above the Sand Wash launch site. Depending on where you took off, the trip takes 30 to 50 minutes. Enjoy the spectacular view of the canyons, mesas, and buttes in the area. From the air, it does indeed look like a desolate and remote river surrounded by canyon after canyon.

From the landing site, a trail leads northeast over to the edge of the butte and winds down to the river and launch site. It's an 800-foot drop to the river over approximately 2 miles. At Sand Wash there is a historic cabin, a BLM ranger station, and a mesh hut for staying clear of bugs. The water is slow moving here, and the bugs can be ferocious the first day out. Many outfitters use a small outboard motor to get quickly downstream the first day. This is something private parties may want to consider as well.

An evening camp on a sandy beach completes day one. With an outboard motor you should be able to cover about 27 miles.

DAY 2: Today you face Big Canyon Rapid, Firewater Rapid, and Cedar Ridge Rapid. And just before river mile 63 you come to a panel of petroglyphs on river right. The east-facing panel can be found a quarter mile up the trail. Flat Canyon Rapid shows up shortly after the petroglyph panel.

Kids love the driftwood for sculptures, and the sandy beaches are great for castles and other building projects. The children I've seen on this river trip spent extensive time engineering little sand dams and waterways down the hillside at camp. Evenings are their time to play. Water fights with squirt guns and cannons help break up the flat-water sections. Near the end of the day you come to Steer Ridge, the first Class III rapid on the trip.

DAY 3: Surprise Rapid, Rock Creek Spring, and Rock Creek Ranch are the order of the day. At river mile 54 a cool, clear stream runs from a side canyon on river right. We dunked ourselves in the chilling waist-deep water and hiked the trails leading farther back into the canyon. This is a great place to top off your water containers.

The area above the stream is the beginning of Rock Creek Ranch, a historic ranch built in the early 1900s by the Seamounton brothers. The land has been cleared and flattened. The ranch still has the original home structure, with outbuildings, old equipment, and bits of glass, rusty furniture, and old leather boots. A child's wagon and some old iron tools sit next to the shed. The house was built by hand from rock found in the canyons.

There is a good campsite just before river mile 40.

DAY 4: Start with a visit to the McPherson Ranch at mile 39.5 on river left. The ranch was started by Jim McPherson in 1890 and includes the remains of a hotel built in the 1970s. McPherson often swapped horses to aid Butch Cassidy and his gang of outlaws.

Back on the river, spend the rest of the morning negotiating Florence Creek and Wire Fence Rapids. At mile 37.5 you enter Gray Canyon and hit Three Fords, Last Chance, Range Creek, and Rabbit Valley Rapids to finish out the day.

DAY 5: Today you tackle the largest rapids: Coal Creek, Poverty, Rattlesnake, Nefertiti, Butler, Stone House, Short Canyon, and Swaseys Rapids. It's a fun day of white-water paddling

—a great day to be in a Duckie. The take-out point is shortly after Swaseys Rapid at river mile 12.

Drive south on a dirt road that parallels the river to the town of Green River, and then head back to the Moab airport or home.

RESOURCES

TOURS AND GUIDES

Sheri Griffith Expeditions, Inc. (Moab): 1-800-332-2439; www.griffithexp.com

Moki Mac River Expeditions (Salt Lake City): 1-800-284-7280; mokimac@mokimac.com

Holiday River Expeditions (Salt Lake City): 1-800-624-6323

RAFT AND EQUIPMENT RENTALS

Canyon Voyages: 1-800-733-6007; www.canyonvoyages.com; this may be the only company in Moab that will outfit an entire river trip

MOAB LODGINGS

There are over 1,700 campsites in and around Moab. For more information and reservations call 1-800-748-4386 or e-mail reservations@moab.net. Or try one of the following bed & breakfasts.

Sunflower Hill Bed & Breakfast: 185 N. 300 E. Moab; 1-800-662-2786; www.sunflowerhill.com; charming rooms with surrounding gardens and wooded walkways; laundry facility available; $145–$195

Cali Cochitta, House of Dreams Bed & Breakfast: 110 S. 200 E. Moab; 1-888-429-8112; www.MoabDreamInn.com; lovely gardens and quaint rooms; seasonal rates from $69–$150

USEFUL WEB SITES AND PHONE NUMBERS

Utah BLM river information: www.blm.gov/utah/price/riverinf.htm

Green River Aviation Flight Service: 1-877-597-5479; www.greenriveraviation.com

Redtail Aviation: 1-800-842-9251; www.moab-utah.com/redtail

Slickrock Air Guides: 1-866-259-1626; www.slickrockairguides.com

BLM, Price Field Office: 435-636-3622; www.ut.blm.gov/utah/price

River Runners Shuttle Service (Green River, Utah): 1-800-241-2591; www.desertsw.com

A LITTLE HISTORY, GEOLOGY, FLORA, AND FAUNA

Desolation Canyon is formed from layers of relatively recently exposed sandstone along with bits of limestone. The recession of a prehistoric sea caused the variations in the jagged cliffs and outcroppings. The canyon walls can be geologically categorized into one formation rather than the usual naming of strata. The entire cliff band in Desolation Canyon is known as the Green River Formation. The strata change little throughout the canyon, with a consistent range of color and rock.

Once you enter Gray Canyon the color and age of the rock change. Though no dinosaur remains have been found in Desolation Canyon, Gray Canyon comes from an older time when those giants still roamed the area. Brownish red walls give way to gray, yellow, and white as you go from one canyon to the next. Gray Canyon holds most of the larger rapids.

The area's remote canyons made a perfect hideout for Butch Cassidy and other outlaw bands in the days of the Wild West. After robbing a bank, the outlaws would hightail it into the canyons and find a vantage point that would allow them to see who was following them for miles in any directions. It was an easy escape for them, and a frustrating chase for lawmen. Local historians note that the ranchers found the outlaws far more pleasant to work with than the sheriff and his men.

Seven hundred years before the Wild West era, the ancient Fremont people dominated the central part of Utah. They left behind writings, stone ruins, arrowheads, and pottery to tell their story. Clay figurines dating back 900 years have been found in Range Creek Cave. Tribes of Ute Indians occupied the area when the Dominguez-Escalante Expedition crossed through the Green River country in 1776. Today, the river borders the Uintah and Ouray Indian Reservations to the east, where Native Americans continue to farm and ranch.

On our first day of floating we saw bighorn sheep coming down to the river for a drink. At Rock Creek I found cougar tracks, and every day my son chased lizards along the beaches. Black bear, cougars, coyotes, lizards, midget faded rattlesnakes, canyon wrens, peregrine falcons, red-tailed hawks, turkey vultures, magpies, American avocets, beaver, and river otters are some of the abundant wildlife of the area. Catfish and the endangered Colorado squawfish and humpback chub call the river home. Encounters with black bears have been common in the past few years. Boaters are advised to bearproof their camps.

When you wake from a warm night of sleeping on top of your sleeping bag under a clear sky full of stars, take a moment to look at the tracks of the animals, insects, and amphibians that made their way across the sand overnight. It will remind you that we share space with a world of other life forms. Leave only your footprints in the sand.

Mountains

Red Pine Lake in the Wasatch Mountains

Wasatch Range; Big Cottonwood Canyon and Mill Creek Canyon

MOUNT RAYMOND AND THE WASATCH CREST TRAIL

A View From the Top

Have you ever found yourself on the spine of a high mountain range, with views of row after row of mountains and valleys on one side and evergreens, aspen, and a rainbow of wildflowers framed

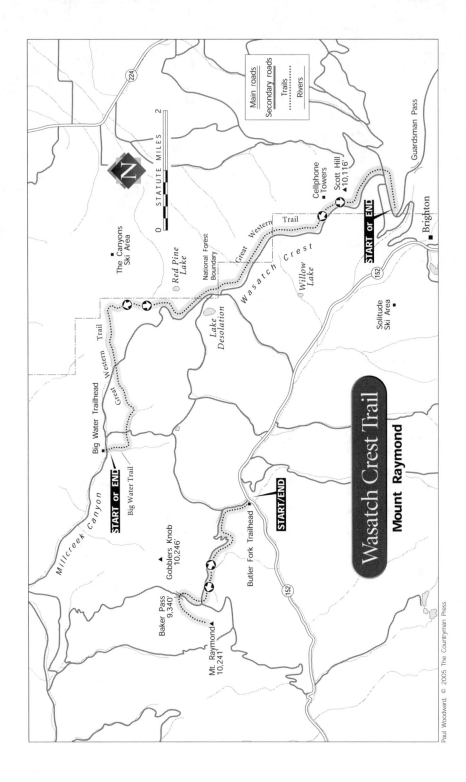

Wasatch Crest Trail
Mount Raymond

Main roads
Secondary roads
Trails
Rivers

N

STATUTE MILES
0   2

224

The Canyons Ski Area

Red Pine Lake

National Forest Boundary

Great Western Trail

Great Western Trail

Big Water Trailhead

START or END

Big Water Trail

Millcreek Canyon

Lake Desolation

Willow Lake

Wasatch Crest

Solitude Ski Area

Cellphone Towers

Scott Hill
▲10,116'

START or END

Brighton

152

Guardsman Pass

Gobblers Knob
10,246'

Baker Pass
9,340'

Mt. Raymond
10,241'

Butler Fork Trailhead

START/END

152

against stark and dramatic peaks on the other? Welcome to Mount Raymond.

Have you ever ridden the range? No, not the buffalo-strewn range of old cowboy songs, the Wasatch Range—the "Backbone of Utah." The trail that runs along the ridge of the mountain between Big Cottonwood Canyon and the Park City area, the trail mountain bikers hail as the premier ride of the Wasatch. Welcome to the Wasatch Crest Trail.

These trails have been chosen for their expansive alpine flavor. Both the hike and the mountain bike involve a solid elevation gain, so neither can be called easy, but getting the "view from the top" has never been about ease. These trails are lush and green with streams nearby and waist-high wildflowers, and both culminate in jaw-dropping scenic views. They offer a strenuous and exciting weekend adventure. For an easier biking option, you can also try the Mill Creek Pipeline Trail. Welcome to the Wasatch Range.

SPORT: Hiking and mountain biking

RATING: Mount Raymond involves strenuous uphill hiking; the Wasatch Crest Trail requires bikers to make a sustained uphill push to the top of the ridge; and the Mill Creek Pipeline Trail is easy to intermediate at low altitude.

DISTANCE: Mount Raymond, 7.5 miles round trip; Wasatch Crest Trail, 13 miles one way with shuttle; Mill Creek Pipeline Trail, 7.2 miles one way with shuttle

TIME: Mount Raymond, six hours; Wasatch Crest Trail, four hours; Mill Creek Pipeline Trail, one hour

GETTING THERE: Mount Raymond. The hike to Mount Raymond starts at Butler Fork Trailhead 8 miles up Big Cottonwood Canyon (UT 190) on the east side of Salt Lake City. Head south from the city on I-15, and then take Exit 302 toward I-215. Merge onto I-215 E via the exit on the left marked Ski Areas. Take Exit 6 (6200 S) for Ski Areas/Solitude/

Brighton/Snowbird/Alta. Turn right onto UT 190 for 1.6 miles, and then left onto Big Cottonwood Canyon Road. The trailhead is 8 miles up canyon on the left side of the road. It's easy to spot and has parking for 10 or so cars.

Wasatch Crest Trail/Guardsman Pass. To reach the Wasatch Crest Trail, drive 14.2 miles up Big Cottonwood Canyon, past Solitude Ski Resort to a sign for Guardsman Pass. Turn sharply to the left. At 0.8 mile you pass through a red metal gate, and a mile later you come to a dirt road on the left at a sharp hairpin turn. Park along the hairpin turn and start biking up the dirt road. Just lift your bike over or around the fence. This is not an official trailhead because it crosses private land, but it's regularly used as the starting point for the ride. Be respectful.

To get to the end of the Wasatch Crest Trail ride (where you'll leave a shuttle vehicle), head out on Foothill Boulevard on the east bench of Salt Lake City. Take the 39th South Street exit and proceed to 3800 South. Turn right and head east into Mill Creek Canyon. The Big Water Trailhead is at the top of the canyon, 9 miles from the base. Mill Creek Canyon is open to cars from July 1 through November 1, but you can peddle up the road anytime. All cars that use the canyon must pay a $2.25 fee.

Upper Mill Creek Pipeline Trail. The Upper Mill Creek Pipeline Trailhead is 6.3 miles up Mill Creek Canyon. The trailhead is clearly marked with a sign for Mt. Aire and the Pipeline Trail. The trail to Mt. Aire and Lambs Canyon starts at the obvious trailhead, but the Pipeline Trail you'll be taking is 50 feet or so down canyon. It's easy to spot and parallels the road at the start.

TRAIL: Mount Raymond. The trail to Mount Raymond is absolutely divine. The path is easy to follow; just look for signage to Mill A Basin. At the base of Mount Raymond, about 3 miles in, you come to the first unsigned fork in the trail. Take the right leg and make your way to the saddle between Mount Raymond and Gobblers Knob, where there are three unmarked trail options. Gobblers Knob lies to the northeast and Mount Raymond to the southwest. Follow the small footpath to the west. The trail is packed dirt, which doesn't change until your assault on the

The view of Mount Raymond from the saddle

peak. It then becomes a two-handed ascent up a rocky knife-edge to a giant pile of rocks at the peak.

The elevation at Butler Fork Trailhead is 6,900 feet, ascending to 10,241 feet at the top of Mount Raymond. It's a steady climb most of the way, though there are meandering stretches through groves of aspen and wildflowers. One of the loveliest places in the Wasatch Range, this path is not only about sitting on the summit—although that is grand—but also reveling in the journey. Once on top, you have a view of Big Cottonwood Canyon to the south and Mill Creek Canyon, adjoining canyons, and downtown Salt Lake City to the north. The views and the solitude make the climb well worth the effort.

Wasatch Crest Trail. The Wasatch Crest Trail is one of the premier mountain bike routes in the Wasatch Range. Primarily single track that twists its way up to the spine of the Wasatch Range and then along the ridge, the trail offers views of Park City down one side and Mill Creek and her sister canyons down the other. This trail is a portion of the Great Western Trail, which runs 3,000 miles from Mexico to Canada. It is well used and maintained.

The trail can be approached from either side: Guardsman Pass in Big Cottonwood Canyon or Big Water Trailhead in Mill Creek Canyon. Most riders begin at Guardsman Pass and have a shuttle pick them up at the bottom of Mill Creek Canyon. But you can also start at Big Water Trailhead or the base of Mill Creek Canyon and arrange for a shuttle back from Guardsman Pass. If you want to avoid dealing with a shuttle, begin at either end and do the ride out and back.

If you start at Guardsman Pass you face an insane uphill for 2 or 3 miles. Part of this climb is aptly named Puke Hill, but it's the quickest way to the ridgeline and will give you more downhill mileage on the way to Big Water Trailhead. The trail starts as a dirt road on land owned by the Salt Lake City Water Department. You also cross sections of land owned by the Utilities Department, several mining companies, and the Forest Service. Gates and signs along the way demonstrate to all riders that the landowners have the option of denying access, but the unofficial trailhead at Guardsman Pass has been used for many years as an access point for the Wasatch Crest Trail. Bathrooms will soon be installed at this trailhead.

When you enter the Wasatch–Cache National Forest the double track turns to hard-packed single track. The elevation at the top is 9,900 feet. A note of caution: The "spine" just above Desolation Lake has unseated many an expert rider. Expect to walk your bike here. The ridgetop has many sections that require attention and skill, but you'll like the speed of the downhill. The ridge ride is what you've come for, so enjoy the personality of the trail. If riding on a Saturday prepare to encounter a hiker or two. Dogs are allowed in the Mill Creek section at all times, and bikes are allowed only on even calendar days (e.g., 2nd, 4th, etc.).

If you start at Big Water Trailhead, you have 7 miles of uphill with a shorter section of downhill on the Guardsman Pass side. Again, bikes are only allowed in Mill Creek Canyon on even calendar days. When traveling this direction you come to a couple of unmarked junctions with spur trails. The first is located after a bridge, where three trails converge on the main trail (UTM 12 T 0445439/4502938; elevation 8,122). Follow the main trail up and around the stream to the left, ignoring the spur trails that come in on the south side of the stream.

At signed junctions, follow markers for the Great Western Trail and Desolation Lake. After you exit Mill Creek Canyon (a sign announcing that bikes are allowed only on even days marks the boundary), the trail from Park City will join from the left (UTM 12 T 0449181/4504175; elevation 8,919). Unless you're heading to Park City, continue up and to the right to Desolation Lake, the top of the ridge, and eventually the National Forest boundary, the cell phone towers, and the descent to Guardsman Pass.

Taking the trail out and back from either trailhead gives you a 20-mile ride with plenty of up and down in each direction. If you're riding from the Big Water Trailhead, you can make the ride a little shorter and easier by not descending Puke Hill. Just turn around at the National Forest boundary and cell phone towers, which gives you a nice long ride up and then a descent on the way back.

Upper Mill Creek Pipeline Trail. The Upper Mill Creek Pipeline Trail starts out parallel to the road and rolls pleasantly down canyon, offering a great view of Mill Creek and the surrounding mountains. The trail descends almost imperceptibly in spots, between nice winding downhill jaunts. It's a dirt single track through lush hardwood trees and

Biking the Wasatch Crest Trail

grasses, opening to a view of the canyon every now and then. It's a south-facing route, so it clears of snow early.

By starting at the upper trailhead and riding down canyon to the Lower Pipeline Trailhead, you cover 7 miles, with the option of continuing out past Rattlesnake Gulch to the View Point and back. If you ride this extra spur to the overlook you are rewarded with a view of the entire Salt Lake Valley. Add an extra 2 miles out and back for this spur. A shuttle is necessary for the Pipeline Trail.

△ CAMPING: The drive up Mill Creek Canyon takes you into the beautiful Wasatch–Cache National Forest. In many places the road is covered with a canopy of trees, and there are plenty of picnic areas available on the way to the Big Water Trailhead. Big Water has an outhouse but no running water. The only amenity at Guardsman Pass is the newly installed outhouse.

The Salt Lake Ranger District has three campgrounds up Big Cottonwood Canyon (UT 190): Jordan Pines, Spruces, and Redman. Jordan Pines is located about 8.8 miles up the canyon. Turn right on Cardiff Fork Road. The entrance is about 0.25 mile off the main highway on the east side of the road. It's open from May to mid-October, and vault toilets and garbage receptacles are provided. Camping at Jordan Pines is by reservation only.

Big Cottonwood Canyon is within the Salt Lake City watershed, so special restrictions apply and are strictly enforced. No domestic animals are permitted in Big Cottonwood Canyon, and this includes the campgrounds. Fires are allowed in fire rings only, and you should plan on bringing your own firewood.

Spruces Campground is 9.7 miles up Big Cottonwood Canyon and is open from the end of May to mid-October. Spruces is the largest campground on the Salt Lake Ranger District. It has 97 campsites with tables, grills, and fire circles. Water faucets are located throughout the campground. Flushable vaulted rest rooms and central garbage receptacles are provided.

Redman Campground is 13 miles up Big Cottonwood Canyon and is open mid-June to the end of September. Redman has 43 campsites with tables, grills, and fire circles. Water faucets are located throughout the campground (though there is no water on the eastern end of the loop between sites 41 and 42). Vault toilets and a central garbage receptacle are provided. There are no RV hook-ups, and most sites are first come, first served. Camping is allowed only in designated spots, and backpackers must establish all camps 200 feet from any water source.

SEASON: The season generally runs from mid-June through mid-October, although in some years the snow melts a little later in the season and access is restricted into July or August. But that is the exception to the rule.

PERMITS: None necessary.

FEES: There is a vehicle fee of $2.25 upon leaving Mill Creek Canyon.

CLOTHING AND EQUIPMENT: Bug repellant is highly recommended on all these routes. There are plenty of little critters in the lush alpine environs that want to suck your blood. Mountain bikers should be prepared to fix tires and perform routine maintenance. It's often possible to get cell phone reception along the entire Wasatch Crest ride because of the towers on the ridge, so bring your phone in case of emergency. Make sure you have plenty of water and food to keep your energy high. If it's a warm day you may want sunscreen and sunglasses.

SUGGESTED ITINERARY

DAY 1: Hike to Mount Raymond and enjoy a picnic on the summit. Camp at one of the campgrounds in Big Cottonwood Canyon.

DAY 2: Bike the Wasatch Crest and/or Mill Creek Pipeline Trails, then rest up and exchange leg massages.

RESOURCES

BIKE RENTALS

Canyon Sports LTD: 1844 E. Ft. Union Blvd. near the mouth of Big Cottonwood
Canyon; 801-942-3100

Wasatch Touring: 702 East 100 South, Salt Lake City; 801-359-9361;
wtouring@xmission.com

USEFUL WEB SITES AND PHONE NUMBERS

Reservations for campsites can be made through the National Recreation Reservation
Service at 1-877-444-6777 or at reserveusa.com.

Wasatch-Cache National Forest: 3285 East 3300 South, Inside REI, Salt Lake City;
Tuesday–Saturday, 10:30 AM–7 PM; 801-466-6411; www.fs.fed.us/r4/wcnf

A LITTLE HISTORY, GEOLOGY, FLORA, AND FAUNA

Over 60 percent of the water used by Salt Lake City residents comes from the Wasatch Mountains. Due to the heavy dependence upon this water system there are many laws in place to keep the area clean. Dogs and other domestic animals are not allowed in watershed areas—including Big Cottonwood Canyon—without permits. Mill Creek Canyon isn't part of the Salt Lake watershed system, so it's dog-walking heaven. Expect to run into dogs on every trail.

No human excreta can be deposited within the city watershed area except in approved toilets, and camping is allowed only in designated campgrounds. This doesn't apply to backpacking, but backpackers must camp over 200 feet from the nearest water source. Bathing and swimming or washing anything in the springs, marshes, or streams is prohibited.

During this weekend adventure you will find yourself in the Wasatch-Cache National Forest, and this section, the Wasatch National Forest, was officially designated in 1906. The total forest covers nearly 1.2 million acres and is composed of high desert and alpine landscapes, pristine lakes and streams, and rugged mountain peaks. More than 318,000 acres are in designated wilderness areas, and this limits human uses to foot traffic and prohibits any man-made structures. Congress set these wilderness areas aside to remain unspoiled for future generations and to protect the vital resources that were overgrazed and heavily logged by the first settlers.

Wasatch is a Ute word meaning "low place in high mountains." Because of the abundance of fish and wildlife, the Utes, Fremont, and Shoshoni Indians all lived in the valleys of northern Utah. The first trappers and explorers, such as Jim Bridger, Kit Carson, and Jedediah Smith, made their way to these canyons and mountains in the 1820s. And of course the first permanent group of settlers arrived in 1847 when the Mormon leader Brigham Young said, "This is the place." After a cross-country trek to flee religious persecution, the Mormons made the Salt Lake Valley their home.

The early pioneers used trees and rock from the mountains to build their homes and places of worship. They used the waters to irrigate their crops and raise livestock. Even the rocks used in the construction of the Salt Lake Temple were quarried from mountain outcroppings.

White Pine Lake

Bear River Range, Logan Canyon

WHITE PINE AND
TONY GROVE LAKES

A Cache Valley Sampler

The trail to White Pine Lake—located near Mount Naomi, the highest peak in the Bear River Range—has been in use for almost a hundred years. It's alpine hiking at its most beautiful. Stands of fir, spruce, and aspen surround this glacial lake, which is framed by a cirque of cliffs. During July and August the mountain meadows are covered in a carpet of colorful wildflowers. A hike here envelops you in solitude,

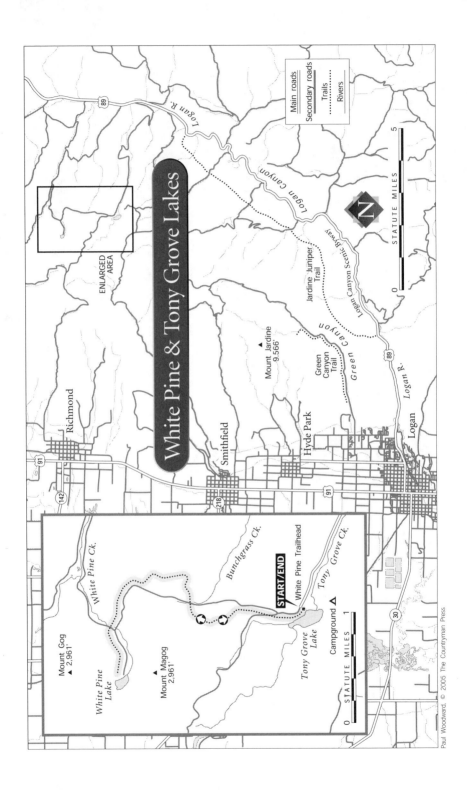

White Pine & Tony Grove Lakes

Main roads
Secondary roads
Trails
Rivers

ENLARGED
AREA

Logan R.

Logan Canyon

Jardine Juniper Trail

Logan Canyon Scenic Byway

Green Canyon Trail

Green Canyon

Mount Jardine
9,566'

Richmond

Smithfield

Hyde Park

Logan

Logan R.

N

STATUTE MILES
0   5

Mount Gog
▲ 2,961'

White Pine Ck.

White Pine Lake

Mount Magog
▲ 2,961'

Bunchgrass Ck.

START/END

White Pine Trailhead

Tony Grove Ck.

Tony Grove Lake

Campground ▲

STATUTE MILES
0   1

Paul Woodward. © 2005 The Countryman Press

and you'll enjoy the magical flight of hummingbirds that come to share lunch. It's an easy packing trip among some of the tallest peaks in the range, and the trailhead at Tony Grove is next to another calm lake that's perfect for an afternoon of canoeing and picnicking.

The trailhead is accessible through Logan Canyon, which is home to an array of top-notch mountain biking trails as well. The Jardine Juniper Trail is one of the most popular intermediate trails in the canyon. It takes you to a famous juniper tree of the same name that's estimated to be 1,500 to 3,200 years old. The trail runs along a stream and the path of several winter avalanches, and there is an outstanding variety of trees and flowering plants that are especially colorful in the fall. Used by hikers and mountain bikers, it's a moderate to strenuous ride that requires some technical skill on switchbacks and rocky terrain.

The Green Canyon Trail, which is accessed a few miles to the north, is a better trail for novice bikers. This area is especially scenic in late spring and early fall. A cave near the picnic area was used by Native Americans many thousands of years ago, and rock from the area was quarried out in pioneer days for the LDS temple and tabernacle in the city of Logan.

SPORT: Backpacking, camping, mountain biking, canoeing

RATING: White Pine Lake Trail, easy; Jardine Juniper Bike Trail, moderate; Green Canyon Bike Trail, easy; Tony Grove Lake, casual canoeing

DISTANCE: White Pine Lake Trail, 3.5 miles one way; Jardine Juniper Bike Trail, 5.8 miles one way; Green Canyon Bike Trail, 3.8 miles one way with the option of going farther

TIME: Two days for White Pine Lake; one for the Jardine Juniper or Green Canyon Trails

GETTING THERE: From Salt Lake City, head north on I-15 for approximately 54 miles. Take Exit 364 for US 91/1100 South toward US

89/Logan/Utah State University. Take the ramp toward Brigham City and continue straight, which will lead you into Sardine Canyon up US 91 north. The canyon is 26.5 miles long and ends at Logan where US 91 turns into Logan's Main Street. Follow it to 400 North, and then turn east. The mouth of Logan Canyon is on the east side of town, and 400 North will take you straight there.

White Pine Lake Trail. About 22 miles up the canyon, turn left at the sign for Tony Grove Lake and Campground. It's a 7-mile drive to the lake on a paved road. There are rest rooms at the parking area, and the trailhead to White Pine Lake is on the north side of the parking lot. The drive from Salt Lake City to Logan takes 1.5 hours and covers 82 miles. It's another half-hour to Tony Grove.

Jardine Juniper Trail. The Jardine Juniper Trail is located about 12 miles up Logan Canyon. A sign on the left indicates where to turn off the main road. You can't see the sign until you're right on it, so watch the mileage. Turn left at Wood Camp and cross the bridge, following the dirt road a few hundred yards to a small parking area at the trailhead. Parking here is free.

Green Canyon Trail. To reach Green Canyon, head north on Logan's Main Street. Turn east on 1400 North and follow it 2.2 miles as it winds up the hill, where it changes to 1500 North. Turn north at the stop sign on 1600 East. (You will enter North Logan.) Finally, turn east on 1900 North and follow this road 1.4 miles to the trailhead.

▐ TRAIL: White Pine Lake Trail. The White Pine Lake Trail starts on the north side of the parking lot at Tony Grove Lake. The trail climbs 0.25 mile to a backcountry sign-in ledger. This junction is also the Naomi Peak Trailhead. Head to the right and continue up the trail through meadows of spruce and limber pine. In early August the wildflowers are out in abundance, dotting the landscape with soft color.

After 2.1 miles, the trail begins its descent into the White Pine Basin. There is a junction at the bottom with signs directing you toward the lake, campsites, or the Bunchgrass Trail. The campsites are on the northeast side of the lake. Situated between Mounts Magog and Gog, both at 9,700 feet, the lake is shallow and green with magnificent stands of

On the trail

spruce. There are rough trails around the lake, and unlimited alpine areas to explore.

Jardine Juniper Trail. The Jardine Juniper Trail includes 5.8 miles (one way) of intermediate mountain biking with an elevation gain of

Canoeing at Tony Grove Lake

1,800 feet (5,400–7,200 feet). It's a fairly strenuous climb. The trail crosses a bridge near the beginning, with occasional stream crossings as you make your way to the top. The first couple of miles have loose rocks that require a bit of gear shifting. A switchback section follows. When the trail finally turns south, just drop to a lower gear and grind up to the wilderness sign. Continue straight. Near the top of the ridge at mile 4.8 you can turn left to arrive at the Jardine Juniper, or you can continue to the south for views of the valley on a trail that is only 0.2 mile longer.

Green Canyon. The Green Canyon Trail is a combination of single track and backcountry road—perfect for beginners. The parking area has a rest room. Two boulders, one on each side of the trail, make the single track easy to locate. You ride through groves of trees and open meadows, alternating between gravel and dirt. The single track converges with a road after a mile, and you follow the road east for the remainder of the trail, which totals 3.8 to 4 miles. This ride ends at the

Mount Naomi Wilderness boundary fence, but you can also continue following the road to the north. It's rock and gravel with some compact dirt sections. There are picnic areas with tables along the single-track portion of the trail.

MAXIMUM GROUP SIZE: No commercial guides are allowed in the Wasatch-Cache National Forest, but groups fewer than 75 are not regulated for size. In general, Leave No Trace principles suggest group sizes no larger than 12.

CAMPING: There are 10 primitive established campsites at White Pine Lake. We found plenty of room to set up camp here, with large logs available as tables and seats. An outhouse, built as an Eagle Scout project some years ago, is available and marked with a sign. All water needs to be filtered or carried in. Camping is free.

There is a beautiful alpine campground with 37 sites back at Tony Grove Lake. Each site is surrounded by tall evergreens and has picnic tables, fire pits, and pit toilets. These sites are $12 a night. Reservations can be made by calling 1-877-444-6777.

Logan Canyon has many other campgrounds, and costs vary. Free camping is also available in Green Canyon.

SEASON: The highest point on the White Pine Trail is 8,840 feet. For this reason, the summer months are the most pleasant. In early spring, the road to Tony Grove is often still snowed in. July and August also yield the best display of wildflowers. (Please remember to leave these for others to enjoy.) The trail stays open into the fall, although the nights can be chilly.

PERMITS: No permits are required; just sign in on the backcountry register. Groups of 75 or more must contact the ranger station at the mouth of Logan Canyon.

FEES: The fee to use the Tony Grove parking lot is $3 a day or $10 a week. Some of the campgrounds in the area also charge a fee.

CLOTHING AND EQUIPMENT: Bring a light jacket, as the evenings can be cooler at this elevation. I was glad I had a pair of fleece pants for the evenings as well. Giardia is a serious concern in all backcountry streams and lakes, and White Pine and Tony Grove Lake are no exceptions, so filter all water. Insect repellant is always a good idea.

When biking, always carry tools and extra tires. It's never fun to walk your bike out. If you want to canoe at Tony Grove, you'll need to bring your own boat, PFDs, and paddles.

SUGGESTED ITINERARY

DAY 1: Park at Tony Grove Lake and head into the backcountry. You can cover the 3.5 miles to White Pine Lake in the morning, and then have the afternoon and evening free to set up camp and enjoy the environs around the lake.

DAY 2: Spend a leisurely morning over breakfast and explore the trails around the lake. There are plenty of high peaks in the area to choose from. When you make it back to Tony Grove, unload your canoe and spend an hour or two paddling around the lake. You can sometimes spot beaver and muskrat on the north side, and the lake is stocked with rainbow trout. There are picnic sites if you want to have dinner at the lake. Camp at Tony Grove tonight or at another campground down canyon.

DAY 3: Head to the Jardine Juniper or Green Canyon Trailheads. Spend the day mountain biking and enjoying the scenic areas within Logan and Green Canyons.

RESOURCES

BIKE RENTALS
Al's Cyclery and Fitness: 435-752-5131
Joyride Bikes: 435-753-7175

CANOE RENTALS

The Trailhead: 435-753-1541

USEFUL WEB SITES AND PHONE NUMBERS

Utah Trails: www.utahtrails.com/whitepinebear.html

Wasatch-Cache National Forest: www.fs.fed.us/wcnf/

Logan Ranger District: 435-755-3620

Cache Valley Tourist Council: 1-800-882-4433

National Recreation Reservation Service (Tony Grove campsite reservations):
   1-877-444-6777

A LITTLE HISTORY, GEOLOGY, FLORA, AND FAUNA

The highest peaks in northern Utah's Bear River Range are found within the Mount Naomi Wilderness Area along Logan Canyon. This is some of the most beautiful and rugged terrain in the state. Good trail access makes it easy to take day hikes as well as extended backpacking trips. With half a dozen peaks over 9,500 feet, it's literally possible to explore the area for weeks. In 1989 the highway through Logan Canyon (US 89) was designated as a National Forest Scenic Byway. This road begins on the east edge of Logan and winds its way through the mountains to Bear Lake.

Limestone and dolomite are the primary rock types in the area. The bottom third of the canyon has vertical limestone cliffs, which gradually roll into aspen-covered hills. There are many interesting caves, caverns, and depressions, the result of erosion within the limestone.

On the drive through the canyon you can see 300 million years of accumulated rock layers, and you can still find sea fossils and shells that date back hundreds of millions of years. About 70,000 years ago, during the last ice age, a giant shallow sea known as Lake Bonneville came into existence. The Great Salt Lake is the only remnant of this ancient sea. Just 18,000 years ago Bonneville reached 5,150 feet, with a surface area of 20,000 square miles. Eventually it overflowed its basin through Red Rock Pass to the north. The flood of water is said to have been four to five times greater than the flow of the Amazon River. Forming a gorge, it swept through the Snake River drainage and out to the Pacific. The site of the Shoshone Indian Massacre is near this drainage spot.

For thousands of years Native Americans called Cache Valley home, and in the early 1800s mountain men trapped beaver in the mountains and streams here. Several of their annual rendezvous trading celebrations took place here. Cache Valley received its name from the caches of pelts the mountain men pulled from the area.

Today moose, elk, and mule deer have replaced the woolly mammoth and musk ox. Cougar are becoming more common in the area, and birds such as the red-tailed hawk, hairy woodpecker, violet-green swallow, Clark's nutcracker, Steller's jay, magpie, American kestrel, dipper, and broad-tailed hummingbird make the area home.

During July and August the blue penstemon, coralbells, elephanthead, Indian paintbrush, Jacob's ladder, lupine, and anise sweetroot are among the many wildflowers that dot the hillsides. Engelmann spruce, limber pine, quaking aspen, and subalpine fir are the primary trees in the Tony Grove area, and elderberry, gooseberry, mountain ash, willow and wild rose shrubs form the underbrush.

Utah and Rocky Mountain juniper grow on the dry rocky slopes. Wood Camp, where the old Jardine Juniper Trail begins, has been busy since the 1880s when hundreds of people came to log and mill. Nearly a billion board feet of lumber were cut in these mountains. Obviously, there is very little old growth left in Logan Canyon.

In the 1950s a core sample was taken of the Jardine Juniper pith that showed the tree to be at least 1,500 years old. It's the oldest known Rocky Mountain juniper in the region and is known as the Monarch of the Mountains. It barely clings to life.

Tony Grove Lake, the crown jewel of the Bear River Range, has been a favorite recreating spot since the turn of the last century when rich townspeople bumped up the dusty mountain road to spend their leisure time at the lake's edge. The name "Tony Grove" comes from this set of uptown or "tony" families.

Lakes in the High Uintah Wilderness

High Uintah Wilderness Area

 KINGS PEAK

The Bird's Eye View from Utah's Highest Peak

Kings Peak, the highest mountain in Utah, is little more than a pile of rocks. But the hike to the 13,528-foot, razor-backed summit takes you into the heart of Uintah country, a land of alpine splendor, flowing streams, and beautiful lakes. The view from the top of Utah's highest peak is worth the hard climb, but a peak this notable you have to climb simply, as George Mallory put it, "because it's there."

219

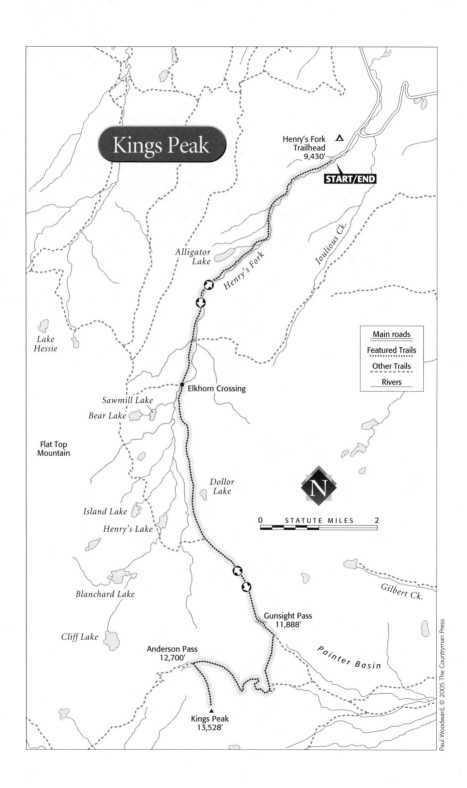

Kings Peak

Henry's Fork
Trailhead
9,430'
START/END

Joulious Ck.

Alligator
Lake

Henry's Fork

Lake
Hessie

Main roads
Featured Trails
Other Trails
Rivers

Elkhorn Crossing

Sawmill Lake
Bear Lake

Flat Top
Mountain

Dollor
Lake

N

0   STATUTE MILES   2

Island Lake
Henry's Lake

Blanchard Lake

Gilbert Ck.

Gunsight Pass
11,888'

Cliff Lake

Painter Basin

Anderson Pass
12,700'

Kings Peak
13,528'

Paul Woodward, © 2005 The Countryman Press

   The Uintah Mountains are home to more than a dozen peaks above 13,000 feet. It's the only major mountain range in the lower 48 states that runs east to west, and it's the largest such range in the western hemisphere. The area around Kings Peak is dotted with over 2,000 glacially carved lakes, many of them full of fish. One of the wettest regions in Utah, the Uintahs provide a large portion of the state's water supply. Because of this, much of the area has a boggy, marshy quality, and serious thunderstorms and incredible lightning are the norm. The Uintahs represent the state's only claim to typical Northern Rockies flora.

   Though you must be in good physical condition, the trip to the top of Kings Peak requires no technical climbing skills—it's completed by groups of Boy Scouts all summer long. Good planning, judgment, and a willingness to scramble up piles of scree will get you to the summit, where you can sign in at the USGS cache box to memorialize your journey.

SPORT: Backpacking, mountaineering, fishing

RATING: The hike to your base camp is moderate, but the actual climb up Kings Peak is strenuous. The total elevation gain from the trailhead to the summit is 4,049 feet (Henry's Fork Trailhead, 9,479 feet; Dollar Lake, 10,785 feet; Gunsight Pass, 11,888 feet; Anderson Pass, 12,700 feet; Kings Peak, 13,528 feet).

DISTANCE: 14.3 miles from Henry's Fork Trailhead to the summit

TIME: Nine or 10 hours of hiking time; two or three days to enjoy the area

GETTING THERE: The drive to the trailhead takes you into southeast Wyoming before bending back into northeast Utah. From Salt Lake City, head east on I-80 toward the Wyoming border. In Wyoming, take Exit 39 south toward the town of Mountain View on WY 414. At Mountain View turn right on WY 410 toward Robertson. WY 410 curves to the west 6.8 miles from Mountain View, while a gravel road (CR 283) continues

Anderson Pass

straight south. Follow the gravel road and enjoy the rolling green hills of aspen and sage. The view occasionally opens to the Uintah peaks.

After approximately 12 miles you come to a fork in the road. The left fork leads to Henry's Fork Trailhead, your destination. The dirt road is well maintained until the Henry's Fork turnoff, where it becomes rough and full of potholes. It's slow going, but still passable for all cars. The first trailhead you come to is for horses and pack animals, so unless you're using animals, continue on another half mile to the hikers' trailhead. Ample parking is available, but the lot is usually packed during the prime season. There's a backcountry information board and sign-in register at the trailhead.

The drive from Salt Lake City to the trailhead takes approximately 2.5 hours.

TRAIL: Numerous trailheads lead to the summit of Kings Peak, but Henry's Fork is the closest and most popular. The trail is well marked and easy to follow, except for a few marshy areas where you need to find your way around pockets of muddy water. Just continue in a southerly direction until you can meet back up with the visible trail. You'll negotiate switchbacks, rocky meadows, and scree piles, and ultimately climb boulder after boulder to the highest one on the pile. Start your attempt on the summit in early morning to avoid the thunderstorms that typically pass over later in the day.

MAXIMUM GROUP SIZE: There is a 14-person limit.

CAMPING: Because this is such a popular area, campsites have been established by continual use. You are backcountry camping, so there are no amenities. Making camp near the base of Kings helps with the early push for the summit. Many people camp around one of the many lakes in the region, but please remember to set up at least 200 feet from any body of water. Much of the area can be marshy and soggy, especially in June and July. If possible, try to use a campsite that has already been established rather than creating a new site. Also, remember to pack out everything that you pack in and leave the site looking as if you've never been there.

SEASON: August is the perfect time of year to tackle Kings Peak unless you want to slide down the snow at Anderson Pass. Snow often lingers through June, and July is fine but wetter than late summer.

PERMITS AND $ FEES: None.

CLOTHING AND EQUIPMENT: Even though August is often the hottest summer month, at these altitudes in the Uintahs you still need your fleece, long underwear, and rain gear. We spent one whole day trapped in the tent by rain and wind, and I was extremely glad I brought a fleece jacket and long pants. Bring a deck of cards or reading material to pass the time when the weather turns bad. Remember to take your rain jacket when you head to the summit; lightning, thunder, and rain are all common. Other suggestions include moleskin and duct tape for blisters and Ibuprofen for muscle aches. And don't forget your water filter.

If you enjoy fishing, bring your gear. The streams and lakes in the Uintahs are known for great fishing.

At the summit there is a USGS cache box where you can take an item and replace it with something you've brought. On the sign-in log people noted that they had exchanged badges, golf balls, candy, insect repellant, and any number of interesting articles.

SUGGESTED ITINERARY

DAY 1: Leave from the Henry's Fork Trailhead. The trail is easy to follow, wandering above a pristine and scenic creek for much of the day. It's the ultimate subalpine experience—the rush of water, wet rocks sparkling in a pine forest. The hike is pleasant and climbs very gradually. About an hour in you come to a sign marked ALLIGATOR LAKE, ELEVATION 9,839. This is the first lake along the route. A 0.4 mile trail leads you to the lake.

Five and a half miles from the trailhead you enter a meadow and junction called Elkhorn Crossing. My group continued south along the Henry's Fork Trail, but if you have more time and want to take in as many lakes as possible you can follow the North

On the summit

Slope Trail to the east. It makes a loop past Bear Lake, Sawmill Lake, Island Lake, Grass Lake, and Henry's Lake, eventually hooking up with the original trail just below Gunsight Pass at the foot of Kings Peak.

Continuing along the Henry's Fork Trail you pass Dollar Lake (elevation 10,785 feet) on your left a couple miles beyond the Elkhorn Crossing junction. We sat at the water's edge here, meditated, and watched a moose forage on the boggy east shore of the lake. Our group hiked 8.7 miles the first day, then set up camp to the east of Henry's Fork Lake in the meadow near the base of the peak.

Spend your evening exploring Henry's Lake and the wonderful waterfalls that grace the area. You have to push through underbrush and over spongy ground, but the falls are well worth it.

DAY 2: Today is summit day. Leave your packs at camp and carry the water, snacks, and essentials—including a rain jacket—in a daypack. Start early in order to miss the afternoon thunder-showers prevalent in the area. And watch for storms as you hike.

The Henry's Fork Trail continues up the northeast side of the peaks (to the left). You are heading through Gunsight Pass at an elevation of 11,888 feet. A long switchback trail takes you to the top of the pass and then drops down again. It may be a bit frus-trating to climb and descend only to climb back up again, but the incredible view softens the blow.

The trail goes around the base of a mountain, with the lakes, marshes, and vast pine forests of Painter Basin visible to the east. When you've made your way to the base of Kings Peak and spot an easy way up, head west and start climbing through the scree fields. There is only a faint trail through the boulder fields, and no trail at all for the last 0.8 mile.

When you've completed this eastern face, your next destina-tion is the top of Anderson Pass, a steep scree-filled slope that shoots down the north side of the mountain back toward camp (elevation 12,700 feet). It sits below Kings Peak, its head right at the base of the boulder pile that leads up to the summit and its base down at the bottom of the mountain. Once you've arrived at Anderson Pass you make your assault on the summit to the south. Pick your way up the larger boulders along the ridge to the top of the peak. Your final destination is obvious.

Enjoy the view from the top and sign in at the register hidden under the highest rock. If the weather looks good, hang out and have a leisurely lunch. If black clouds are moving in, leave the summit immediately and drop down to a safer location.

Back at Anderson Pass, you can cut miles and hours off the return trip by heading directly down the steep scree slope. Although not recommended for hikers with weak ankles, this is a fun way to descend. Once you're at the bottom of the pass, simply walk across the meadow to your campsite.

DAY 3: Beautiful lakes and waterfalls and hundreds of square miles of alpine terrain await your exploration. If you have the time, I highly recommend checking out as much of the Uintahs as possible. If you don't have an extra day, you'll still be able to roam around in the morning before making the five-hour hike back out to the Henry's Fork Trailhead.

RESOURCES

USEFUL WEB SITES AND PHONE NUMBERS
Mountain View Ranger District: 307-782-6555
America's Roof: http://americasroof.com/ut.html; this site offers weather forecasts and links to other Kings Peak sites

A LITTLE HISTORY, GEOLOGY, FLORA, AND FAUNA

The Wasatch-Cache National Forest and High Uintah Wilderness Area are filled with steep canyons and rugged mountain peaks. The Uintahs are the highest mountain range in Utah. The range was formed by subterranean pressure that forced quartzite, sandstone, and shale to the surface some 600 million years ago. In alpine areas above 11,000 feet, the peaks are built of rock and talus, but the subalpine region is rich with lodgepole pine, aspen, and multiple species of willow.

As you gain elevation, Engelmann spruce and subalpine fir appear on the slopes, along with mule deer, moose, and elk. Every two or three years, somebody spots a cougar or a black bear at lower elevations where food is more readily available. Marmots, gray squirrels, red-tailed hawks, and goshawks also call the Uintahs home. And in the multitude of lakes and rivers carved by glaciers during the Pleistocene era you can find beaver and various species of fish, primarily brook and cutthroat trout.

Though the Uintahs are a designated wilderness area, grazing is still allowed. The Forest Service knows that grazing in otherwise pristine areas is controversial, and they do their best to manage the range.

Grazing starts around the first week of July and continues through the end of August or first week of September. If you don't want to share space with the sheep, call the Forest Service office to check which allotments will be in use when you plan to visit. Livestock have grazed in the Uintahs since the late 1800s, although the number of sheep currently allowed is much smaller than it used to be.

Riding the Thunder Mountain Trail

Brian Head

Tantalizing Downhill in "America's Highest Little Resort Town"

Known as one of the best summer mountain biking destinations in the country, Brian Head offers a network of downhill and cross-country single track served by lift and shuttle. It's a small ski resort (population 150) located near Cedar Breaks National Monument in the mountains of southern Utah. With a base elevation of 9,700 feet, it's the highest resort in the state.

There are over 100 miles of challenging single- and double-track trails through aspen forests and green meadows—every one a mountain

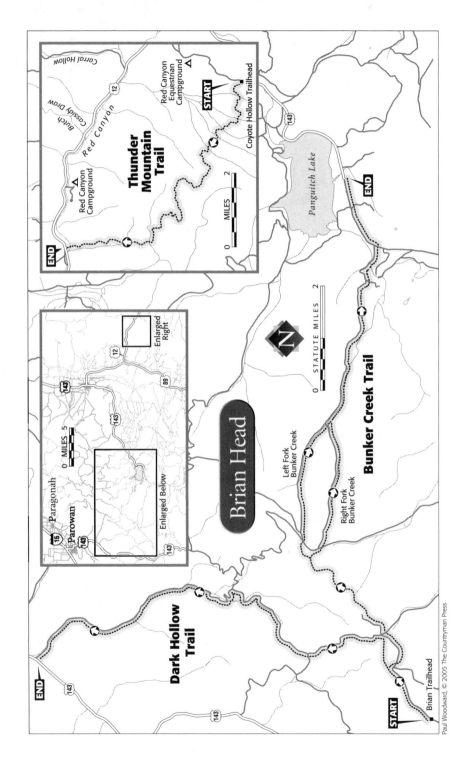

Thunder Mountain Trail

Corral Hollow

Butch Cassidy Draw

Red Canyon

12

Red Canyon Campground

END

Red Canyon Equestrian Campground

START

Coyote Hollow Trailhead

143

Panguitch Lake

END

MILES
0   2

Paragonah

Parowan

15

143

143

12

89

143

Enlarged Right

Enlarged Below

0   MILES   5

Brian Head

N

0   STATUTE MILES   2

Dark Hollow Trail

END

143

143

143

START

Brian Trailhead

Bunker Creek Trail

Left Fork Bunker Creek

Right Fork Bunker Creek

biker's dream. Due to the high elevation, summer temperatures are pleasant, and the fall colors are unbelievable. You can't claim to have mountain biked Utah without having spent time in the saddle in "America's highest little resort town."

During the summer the ski lift will take you to the top of the mountain for a selection of trails, and local bike shops offer shuttles to many downhill trails around the area. There are a few loop trails that don't require a shuttle, but most do because of all the downhill. Shuttle yourself or make arrangements with one of the bike shops.

The tiny town probably won't have everything you might need during your stay, so stop off for supplies before you head up UT 143. There are three bike shops, a few restaurants, a market or two, lots of condos, a couple of lodges, the ski hill, and enough challenging trails to keep you busy for weeks.

 SPORT: Mountain biking

RATING: Thunder Mountain, strenuous uphill with some technical skill required; Bunker Creek, a moderate downhill ride; Paradise Canyon/ Dark Hollow, advanced downhill requiring good technical skill

DISTANCE: Thunder Mountain, 7.8 miles; Bunker Creek, 11.7 miles; Paradise Canyon/Dark Hollow, 14.5 miles

TIME: Thunder Mountain, 1.5 hours; Bunker Creek, 1.5–2 hours; Paradise Canyon/Dark Hollow, 1.5 hours. (Don't forget to add in loading, unloading, shuttle, and wait time.)

GETTING THERE: From Salt Lake City, head south on I-15 toward Las Vegas. Stay on I-15 for 230 miles, until you reach Exit 78 for UT 143/Parowan. Turn left toward Parowan. Once in town, turn left on Center Street and follow UT 143 for 13 miles to the resort. It's roughly a four-hour drive, covering 245 miles.

The Bunker Creek and Dark Hollow Trails start at the same trailhead. Follow the main road through Brian Head to a brown sign on the left side of the road for Vista Point. Take a left here and follow the dirt

Overlook on the trail leading to the Bunker Creek and Blow Hard rides

road for a mile or so until you come to a pullout on the left. There is an outhouse at the parking area. Both trails start across the street from the parking area on a single track that heads northeast.

Thunder Mountain is 45 minutes from Brian Head. Follow UT 143 east to Panguitch, then head east on Center Street about 6.5 miles. Follow the signs toward Bryce Canyon, turning east onto UT 12 and crossing the Sevier River. Follow the road into Red Canyon and the Dixie National Forest. About 7 miles in, a paved bike path parallels the road up the mountain. From here, continue driving for 7.5 miles and then take a right onto a dirt road, the Fremont ATV Trail. In approximately 2 miles, you arrive at Coyote Hollow Trailhead. A sign at the trailhead leads you to the Thunder Mountain Trail.

TRAIL: All three trails discussed here require a shuttle, as do most trails at Brian Head. These trails are the most fun for intermediate mountain bikers.

Thunder Mountain. Thunder Mountain has a beautiful scenic quality and diverse terrain. It's an easy trail to follow, but you'll have a hard time keeping your eyes on your line because the alpine areas and spectacular red rock formations of southern Utah will vie for your attention. The trail has constant ups and downs—with more uphill than the other two rides—and quick shifting is often required. There's a tight switchback descent, a few technical sections, and a fast and fun mile-long roll out at the end.

The ride ends at the scenic pullout you passed on the right just before the DIXIE NATIONAL FOREST sign on the drive in, so leave a shuttle vehicle here on the way to the trailhead. Many skilled riders consider this their favorite trail in the area.

Bunker Creek Trail. The Bunker Creek Trail is primarily downhill, with some technical sections and a ride out on a fire access road. At the trailhead you'll see a single track heading uphill and a four-wheel-drive road straight ahead. Take the single track. When you come to a set of signs—one pointing to Lowder Pond, one to Dark Hollow—go straight ahead on the trail toward Sidney Peak. When you merge with a double track, bear right and continue straight ahead. Don't take the trail to the right.

On the trail straight ahead you come to a sign indicating trails for Left Fork Bunker Creek and Right Fork Bunker Creek. Both will take you to the same spot, but the trail to the right is rockier and more technical. The trails merge at a dirt road that you follow out to UT 143. Turn left and ride a short distance to a Phillips gas station, where the ride ends. Leave a shuttle vehicle here before the ride or arrange to be picked up.

Dark Hollow/Paradise Canyon. The Dark Hollow/Paradise Canyon ride begins at the same trailhead as Bunker Creek. After 1.5 miles a sign points you to the left, where the Dark Hollow Trail splits off. The trail is all downhill, with plenty of rocks, roots, and jumps. This is a great ride, but it requires advanced technical skill and intermediate endurance. The last 6 miles are on a dirt road, which brings you to UT 143 in Parowan Canyon. Leave your shuttle vehicle at the turnoff marked SECOND LEFT

HAND CANYON approximately 9 miles down canyon from Brian Head or arrange for a shuttle at one of the bike shops in town.

There are other great trails in the area, as well. Blow Hard has great views of Cedar Breaks, with some nice uphill climbs and challenging downhill. It's rated intermediate/advanced. Color Country, accessed via the chairlift, is a good trail for beginner and intermediate riders. It winds around the ski slopes through wildflowers and aspens. The Navajo Lake Loop is an easy ride around Navajo Lake, another good beginner ride. Area bike shops are more than willing to help out with additional trail selections.

OTHER ACTIVITIES: Fishing opportunities are abundant in the area. Try Panguitch Lake, Yankee Meadows Reservoir, or Navajo Lake—just to name a few. Road cycling is also popular here, and there are many hiking trails available.

MAXIMUM GROUP SIZE: The size of your party really only matters if you want discounts on your shuttle service. My group included eight bikers.

CAMPING AND ACCOMMODATIONS: Two campgrounds are available in the immediate area. Sugarloaf Bear Flat is on the right, 1 mile up the road from the Brian Head Mountain Bike Park (bike shop). It has free unimproved camping among the aspens with two outhouses nearby. Use an established campsite.

Cedar Breaks National Monument is 7.7 miles from the Brian Head Mountain Bike Park, on the left. It's a scenic drive past the red rock of Cedar Breaks. Drive straight on UT 143 until it becomes UT 148. Continue on 148 directly to Point Supreme Campground. It has 28 sites that run $12 a night and is open June through September.

If you're looking for something more comfortable try Cedar Breaks Lodge, currently the only full-service facility on the mountain. It's on the right side of the road on the way into town and comes complete with pool, Jacuzzi, weight room, and gift shop. The pool and Jacuzzi are particularly nice after a hard day on the trails. There's also a day spa and a couple of on-site restaurants. Prices change seasonally.

Thunder Mountain Trailhead

SEASON: Summer and fall are the best times. Fall colors peak in mid-September, but the leaves are gone by October. Temperatures usually run in the 70s, even in summer. If you want to avoid the crowds, visit in the fall. It's an ideal time to catch the stark and lively colors of the region. Most biking services close by October.

PERMITS: None necessary.

FEES: Shuttle fees typically range from $8 to $15.

CLOTHING AND EQUIPMENT: Bring your mountain bike, helmet, and tools and tubes for repair. I've known bikers who had to push their bikes on the final 6-mile leg of Dark Hollow because they didn't have a spare tube. Don't forget your hydration system, and if you bike in the fall, remember to bring clothing you can layer. The early mornings can be much cooler than the afternoons. Take some energy gel or snacks to keep you strong on the trail, and throw in a camera to catch some great action and scenery shots.

SUGGESTED ITINERARY

DAY 1: Arrive at Brian Head and secure your campsite or accommodations. Bunker Creek makes a good warm-up ride. Then rest up for day two and make your way around to some of the scenic overlooks in the Bryce Canyon area.

DAY 2: If you ride hard you can take in two or three rides today. The trip to Thunder Mountain requires extra travel time so it's best to schedule it when you have a full day. Upon your return, Dark Hollow is a nice hard workout.

DAY 3: Continue to ride or enjoy some of the area's trails on foot. Stop at any bike shop in town for recommendations and trail maps.

RESOURCES

SHUTTLES AND BIKE RENTALS
Brian Head Mountain Bike Park: 435-677-3101; www.brianhead.com
Brian Head Sports: 435-677-2014
Georg's Bike Shop: 1-888-677-2013

USEFUL WEB SITES AND PHONE NUMBERS
Brian Head Chamber of Commerce: 1-888-677-2810; www.brianheadchamber.com
Cedar Breaks National Monument: www.nps.gov/cebr
Cedar Breaks Lodge: 1-888-AT-CEDAR; www.cedarbreakslodge.com

A LITTLE HISTORY, GEOLOGY, FLORA, AND FAUNA

Brian Head sits atop the Markagunt Plateau right next to Cedar Breaks National Monument, established in 1933. They're so close that you can pass from one to the other without even knowing it. The base elevation at the ski hill is 9,700 feet, with peak elevation at 11,307. The subalpine terrain in the mountains and the great red rock amphitheater of Cedar Breaks offer a unique mix of scenery.

The variety is eminently pleasing. High-country ponds, like Alpine Pond, and forests of Engelmann spruce, subalpine fir, and quaking aspen surround the resort town. Starting in late June, lush meadows in the area display colorful Indian paintbrush, blue columbine, shooting star, fleabane, and wild rose. Deer, elk, marmot, fox, coyote, the occasional mountain lion, and black bear all live here, along with Clark's nutcrackers, violet-green swallows, and the common raven.

The Cedar Breaks amphitheater is shaped like a coliseum, 2,000 feet deep and more than 3 miles across. Stone spires, arches, and columns worn by ice, wind, and rain impress with their grand formations and striking color. Iron and manganese give the rock its different reds, yellows, and darker hues. Four amphitheater overlooks are located along UT 143, and each gives a different awe-inspiring perspective.

The surrounding Dixie National Forest contains several old volcanic vents and the black remains of lava in places, along with bristlecone pines, one of the oldest known trees. The fall colors in the area rival those of New England.

Park City/Deer Valley

A Never-Ending Oasis of Trails

Trails that go up, down, sideways, and across. Trails that go under, through, and in between. Trails that are accessible by lift, bike, and shuttle. Park City has all these and more. Recognized internationally, Deer Valley is one of the top 10 mountain bike destinations in the country. The Park City area is home to over 300 miles of biking and hiking trails, with more in the works as the community buys land to build

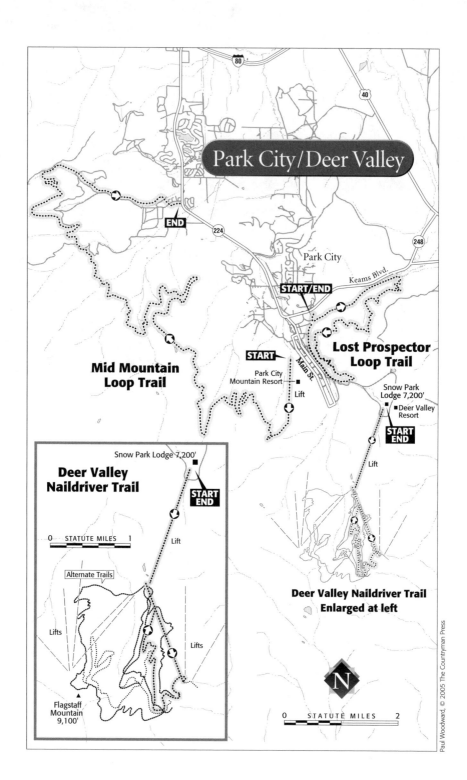

Park City/Deer Valley

END

224

Park City

START/END

Keams Blvd.

248

40

80

Mid Mountain Loop Trail

START

Park City Mountain Resort

Main St.

Lift

Lost Prospector Loop Trail

Snow Park Lodge 7,200'

Deer Valley Resort

START END

Lift

Deer Valley Naildriver Trail

Snow Park Lodge 7,200'

START END

0 STATUTE MILES 1

Lift

Alternate Trails

Lifts

Lifts

Flagstaff Mountain 9,100'

Deer Valley Naildriver Trail Enlarged at left

N

0 STATUTE MILES 2

Paul Woodward, © 2005 The Countryman Press

additional natural trails and restricts development to maintain the natural quality of this mountain resort town.

Prime alpine trails for mountain bikers of all skill levels draws riders here in spring, summer, and fall. Lifts at the three local ski resorts are available to take you to the top for some downhill thrills, but there are many trails where you can just get on and ride. Accommodations range from campgrounds to bed & breakfasts to fancy lodges where you can relax in a hot tub after a day of riding. There is an abundance of swanky restaurants available, or you can pull out the ol' one-burner stove and cook up ramen noodles at camp.

Here, we'll look at three well-loved trails in the area: Mid Mountain Trail, Lost Prospector, and Naildriver. But there are many more. Local bike shops can help you pinpoint an array of options, as well as give you the latest Park City trail map.

 SPORT: Mountain biking

RATING: Mid Mountain Trail, intermediate; Lost Prospector, beginner to intermediate; Naildriver, intermediate with some technical downhill

DISTANCE: Mid Mountain Trail—10.5 miles from the Park City lift to The Canyons Resort gondola; 18.2 miles from the Spiro Trailhead to the base of The Canyons Resort; 25 miles for the loop from Park City. Lost Prospector—7-mile loop from the Rail Trail. Naildriver—2.1 miles from the top of the Sterling Lift at Deer Valley.

TIME: Mid Mountain Trail—2 hours using the Park City lift, longer for other options; Lost Prospector—1 hour; Naildriver—30 minutes

GETTING THERE: From Salt Lake City, head east on I-80 through Parleys Canyon for 26 miles to Exit 2 for Park City. Then turn right onto UT 224 at Exit 145, Kimball Junction/Park City. It's 6 miles to Park City and two more to Deer Valley. For Deer Valley, turn left onto Deer Valley Drive from UT 224. Continue straight until you reach Snow Park Lodge and the Silver Lake Express Lift. The ticket window is right at the front of the lodge.

To reach the Park City Mountain Resort, continue on UT 224, turn right on Empire Avenue, and follow the signs to the lodge. Lift tickets can be purchased at the lift-ticket window on the back side of the lodge.

To reach the Spiro Trailhead, turn right onto Empire Avenue from Park Avenue/UT 224, turn right again onto Silver King Drive, and right yet again at the next stop sign (Three Kings). Turn left on Crescent Road and follow it past the chinked log buildings and around the corner. The Spiro Trailhead is directly on your right. Currently, there is no parking allowed at the trailhead, so you'll have to shuttle the riders and bikes or park along an adjacent road.

The starting point for the Lost Prospector Loop is the Rail Trail off Bonanza Drive. From Park Avenue/UT 224, turn left on Deer Valley Drive and then left again on Bonanza. The Rail Trail is a paved path off the right side of Bonanza, just south of White Pine Touring. You ride down the Rail Trail for 1 mile before veering onto a trail on the right. Look for the SKID ROW sign. The trail is easy to follow, except where you come to a set of jeep roads heading in a variety of directions. Cross the jeep trails and look for the single track on the other side.

⫙ TRAIL: Mid Mountain Trail. The Mid Mountain Trail covers 10.5 miles if you take Park City's Town Lift to the top of the mountain and The Canyons gondola down at the end of the ride. The trail starts out with a nice climb right off the lift, but levels into a rolling ride with small hills as you make your way across the ridge from the Park City Mountain Resort to the Red Pine Lodge at The Canyons Resort. Total elevation gain is under 500 feet. This is an intermediate trail, with a handful of technical switchbacks, downhill rock and root obstacles, and uphill ummph.

Purchase a one-ride pass from Park City Mountain Resort and get on at either of the Park City lifts. The directions provided here are from the town lift because the line is usually shorter and it connects with the Mid Mountain Trail sooner. (If you're looking for an advanced and intense uphill access to the Mid Mountain Trail, try the Spiro Trailhead.)

Once off the town lift, head directly to the right past the Angle Station, a rectangular building off to the right of the lift, and uphill on

Biking the Lost Prospector Trail

the steep jeep road. At 0.21 mile there is a small trail marker for the Mid Mountain Trail on the right. This is where the single track begins. At 2.11 miles you cross a jeep road and a couple of intersecting trails. The trail continues on the other side. At 2.26 miles the Crescent Mine Grade Trail intersects the Mid Mountain Trail; head right, up the hill.

The Crescent Mine Grade Trail is an alternative access route to the Mid Mountain Trail that is easier than the Spiro Trail and less expensive than buying a lift pass. (Refer to the trail map for additional intersecting information.) At 2.59 miles you come out of the aspen trees into a small clearing where you can see a jeep trail below. This is where the Spiro Trail joins the Mid Mountain Trail. There is also a trail heading up the other side of the hill, the Powerline Trail.

Stay on the single track as it heads back into the aspen grove; it intersects the Spiro Trail farther up. If you need to exit the trail for some reason, you can do so at Spiro. Follow the trail signs for the Mid Mountain Trail when available. At 5.42 miles you come to the Iron Mountain saddle, a meadow clearing just below Iron Mountain directly to the northwest. An additional trail goes to the northeast, and this is the last place you can exit before The Canyons. The Mid Mountain Trail continues through the saddle into the aspens on the other side.

At 7.2 miles, after you've rounded Iron Mountain, the view opens up and you see Sniderville and Kimball Junction below. This is your first glimpse of The Canyons Resort, where the trail eventually ends. Riders often think that they are close to finishing at this point, but the trail doesn't descend directly into The Canyons from here. Instead, it heads deeper into the mountains and through a residential area know as The Colony before bringing you to the Red Pine Lodge at The Canyons gondola.

At 10.5 miles you arrive at the Red Pine Lodge. If you're planning to take the gondola down, time your ride so that you arrive before closing time at approximately 5 PM. When there is still plenty of light for good riding on summer evenings, it's easy to forget that the lifts may be closed. Contact the resort before you leave to check the current closing time.

The Mid Mountain Trail runs at 8,000 to 8,500 feet of elevation and is sometimes referred to as the "8,000-foot trail." If you happen to miss

Wildflowers in Deer Valley

the gondola, the trail continues down to the base of The Canyons Resort, an additional 5 or 6 miles.

Lost Prospector Trail. The Lost Prospector Trail is a pleasant intermediate ride that starts right in Park City off the paved Rail Trail. It climbs at an intermediate level and then runs along the mountain with a view of the city and numerous exit points if needed. This trail is a good warm-up for anyone acclimating to the elevation or for riders with limited time. The many access points also make it a good trail to tackle if you're not sure of the weather.

A dirt single track, Lost Prospector offers a scenic ride through lush vegetation until it drops out onto a paved road at the end. It has a variety of technical challenges, with about 500 feet of ascent and descent and some rolling sections. Glide down the paved roads to the city and back to your vehicle at the Rail Trail a couple of blocks away. The trail is tucked into the trees with a view of the city.

Naildriver. The Naildriver Trail is accessed via the Deer Valley Resort lift. It begins with a fast descent into meadows dotted with wildflowers and aspen groves. It has its share of sharp switchbacks and panoramic views, but it's also the least difficult route down from the Sterling Lift at Deer Valley. You can link this trail with other trails on the Deer Valley route—Deer Camp, Flagstaff Loop, Tour Des Suds, and Team Big Bear—to extend it and make it more challenging. Deer Valley Resort has some of the best, most serious biking in the area.

CAMPING AND ACCOMMODATIONS: Park City is famous for its preservation of historic buildings and sites. One such place, the Washington School Inn, was built in 1889 from locally quarried limestone and was one of the first schools to serve the area. Today it's a plush bed & breakfast with cookies warm from the oven, easy downtown access, and delightful luxuriant surroundings. A hot tub is available for a relaxing soak after a day on your bike. Contact them at 1-800-824-1672 or www.washingtonschoolinn.com. Room rates vary from $105 to $185.

The Woodside Inn is hailed as the techie B&B of Park City. Rooms come complete with DVD players, CD alarm clocks, and dedicated phone and data access, and there are home-cooked breakfasts, elevators to each floor, and private baths with Jacuzzi tubs. It's a very comfortable downtown inn with covered parking. Contact them at 1-888-241-5890, 435-649-3494, or www.woodsideinn.com. Room rates vary from $109 to $149.

Camping is available at the Jordanelle State Park (435-649-9540) east of Park City and at the Wasatch Mountain State Park (435-654-1791) off the east side of the Wasatch Mountains 5 miles north of Heber City. State parks are open from April to October. For state park reservations, call 1-800-322-3770.

SEASON: Lifts operate from mid-June through Labor Day, and continue on weekends through mid-September. Non-lift-assisted trails can be accessed year-round—if you're into riding on snow, which usually arrives in October and November.

PERMITS: None necessary.

FEES: Park City Mountain Resort—$10 for a single-ride pass, $16 for an all-day pass; Deer Valley Resort—$12 for a single-ride pass, $20 for an all-day pass; The Canyons Resort—$14 for a gondola pass. Mountain bike rentals run $26 to $35 for a full day.

CLOTHING AND EQUIPMENT: It's no fun to miss a day of biking because you're pushing your bike down the mountain. Be smart and carry spare tires and the tools to keep your bike in top working order. Always wear a helmet, which is required at the resorts. Bring plenty of water, and on longer rides throw in some food to keep your energy high.

SUGGESTED ITINERARY

DAY 1: The number of trails you ride in a day will depend on the kind of shape you're in. If you need time to acclimate to the elevation, tackle the Lost Prospector Trail or ride the Rail Trail today. Once you feel warmed up, treat yourself to the Naildriver downhill at Deer Valley Resort.

DAY 2: The Mid Mountain Trail, accessed from the Park City lift or one of the other suggested trailheads, is a great project for day two. Depending on your stamina, this may be the only ride you want to take today. If you finish early and are ready for more, the Park City lift gives you access to a labyrinth of connecting trails to explore.

RESOURCES

TOURS AND GUIDES
White Pine Touring: 435-649-8710
Deer Valley Mountain Bike School: 435-645-6648
Utah Escapades: 1-800-268-UTAH

MOUNTAIN BIKE RENTALS AND TRAIL MAPS
White Pine Touring: 435-649-8710; www.whitpinetouring.com
Cole Sport: 1-800-345-2938; www.colesport-usa.com
Deer Valley Resort: 435-615-6281; www.deervalley.com
Jans Mountain Outfitters: 1-800-745-1020; www.jans.com
Park City Mountain Resort: 435-658-5582; www.parkcitymountain.com

A LITTLE HISTORY, GEOLOGY, FLORA, AND FAUNA

Park City is an old mining town. It was born and sustained by the variety of ore found in them thar hills—silver, gold, lead, and zinc. What is now a recreation hotspot was, from 1868 to 1956, a town of railways, talus fields, mining roads, mills, loading stations, drain tunnels, and deep mines with three overhead trams, a red-light district, and a few very rich families. Over $400 million in ore came from the mines around Park City. Because the area was originally settled by miners instead of Mormon pioneers, Park City has a style all its own. Utah is a predominantly Republican state with a reputation for conservative leanings, but Park City has always been strongly Catholic and Democratic.

The first ski resort, Snow Park, was established in 1946 by the mining company. In 1963 a small local ski hill was built into a major resort called Treasure Mountain Resort, now known as Park City Mountain Resort. In 1971 the ski resort was sold and the land leased to the new owners. Unlike most ski resorts in the West, which sit on Forest Service or BLM land, the majority of Park City's mountains are still owned by the mining companies. Deer Valley is a mix of private land and mining land. Silver Lake Chateau in Deer Valley was once a snowmelt lake, but it was drained over a hundred years ago to keep the mine from filling with water.

In 1983 Congress passed legislation authorizing the conversion of old railroad tracks into trails. Over 10,000 miles of trails have been established in the lower 48 states, and the Historic Union Pacific Rail Trail, which spans 28 miles from Park City to Echo, is the first such trail in Utah. The path includes 5 miles of pavement and 23 miles of packed dirt.

Because Park City residents have carefully monitored development, they've been able to maintain the natural beauty and habitat of the mountains. The Mountain Trails Foundation, a nonprofit trails association started around 10 years ago to negotiate between private landowners, county and city governments, and community members, has helped create the area's world-renowned trails. As you ride the trails here you'll find that the lush greenery is not only home to an array of wonderful plant life, but also the yellow-bellied marmot, red-tailed hawk, Uintah ground squirrel, broad-tailed hummingbird, porcupine, sage grouse, sandhill crane, mule deer, golden eagle, mink, moose, snowshoe rabbit, mallard duck, and badger—just to name a few.

Filled with a variety of historic landmarks, pathways, buildings, stage stops, and all the touches of an old mining town, Park City has become a town noted for its preservation of history and natural places. It's a resort town that can cater to your every whim, but it's also a place where you can lose yourself in the color and vitality of alpine fields and abundant flowers. Best of all, hundreds of miles of trails stretch before you, just waiting to take you somewhere wonderful.

Index